PRAISE FOR PAUL DISCLAFANI

"Paul's wry wit in documenting everyday life such as the hierarchy of Christmas tree ornaments, trips to the local barber, and countless other daily transactions makes his essays a must-read."

— GREG, WEST ISLIP, NY

"Paul brings me to the exact spot and same type of people in my earlier life. He has a gift of bringing his readers back to that place in time. He can tell stories so funny and on the nose that you can't put his writings down. What a skilled and funny guy. Always a great read."

— BILL MAHONEY, LEVITTOWN, NY

"Paul's articles have something for everyone. They touch upon everyday issues that we have experienced in the past, as well as present-day issues. Always making lite of the situation, he puts a smile on my face!"

— STEVE DEL CASINO, FLORIDA

"Paul has the ability to open my eyes and make me laugh at the same time."

— WALTER G. HOEFER, THE HAMPTONS, LONG ISLAND

"Paul's writings remind me of another favorite Long Island author, Ed Lowe. Always about home, always true to the heart and always able to relate."

— LISA ANGERMANN, (FORMERLY OF MASSAPEQUA), FORT PIERCE, FLORIDA

"Your articles bring up so many touching memories from my life. I love to see what you are going to write next. What a talent you have to manipulate the English language and turn it into a beautiful story. I have the same words at my disposal that you have, but my writings never come near the level of perfection that yours do. What a lovely gift you have been given! Keep educating and entertaining us!"

— LEAH GASKIN

"Paul DiSclafani truly captures the essence of living on Long Island. His everyman perspective and unique sense of humor make each column a delight to read, whether he is discussing the loss of a pet or a colonoscopy. Long Island's answer to Dave Barry."

— CHRISTINE PRUDENTE, BAYSIDE, NY

"Paul is a fabulous writer. I look forward each week to receiving the newspaper and reading his column. He makes the simplest of topics interesting that has a personal touch that you can associate to, and there is always a bit of humor that brings a smile to your face."

— EILEEN H, OLD BETHPAGE, NY

"I enjoy reading about anything Paul writes. I relate to his stories as I come from the same neighborhood in the East New York section of Brooklyn. Everything he writes is so down-to-earth and descriptive as I feel I'm right there all over again. It warms my heart to have friends that have mutual memories."

— JOANNE K, EAST MEADOW, NY

"Paul is a husband, father, an information technology guru, a fantasy football commissioner, a great neighbor, a very knowledgeable sports and music fan, a former radio/TV host, and everybody's best friend. Oh, and he's a writer too, And a really good one."

— ROY E, WESTFIELD, NJ

"It's harder to write humorously than seriously, especially when it's poking fun at your own life and life's stories. Paul does this effortlessly. Some authors write about their life's merriment in such a narrative that reading them becomes no less than a laugh fest."

— GEORGE S, MASSAPEQUA PARK, NY

"I so enjoy reading Paul's columns. It's like a trip down memory lane to the most wonderful times of our lives. He brings back all the wonderful times with family and friends, painting a beautiful picture. He has a wonderful way with words. I hope he will someday write my obituary, although, God willing, not for a very long time!"

— MARIA B, AMITY HARBOR, NY

"A writer whose commitment to his readers is an exact match of his true self. A totally truthful and enjoyable experience at all times. Paul's writing always leaves you engaged and with a smile on your face no matter the topic."

— **MAUREEN KEHOE, LAKE GROVE, NY**

"I also grew up in Massapequa. Paul's perspective on daily life makes his essays a joy to read."

— **CAROL SIMINOFF, TORTOLA, BVI**

"I enjoy reading Paul's stories in the Massapequa Observer. His stories could be written about my own Italian close-knit family. I sit and smile about all those great memories that come back to life when he writes about them. I have also read his 1st book and all his antics in the 70's and 80's and makes me think about my own teenage years."

— **DONNA, DEER PARK, NY**

"I enjoy Paul's way of bringing a story to life. The way he describes his adventures makes you feel you are on the ride with him!"

— **KIM R, LONG ISLAND**

A Journey Through the Mind of a Newspaper Columnist

Paul DiSclafani

Red Penguin BOOKS

Long Island Living

Copyright © 2021 by Paul DiSclafani

All rights reserved

Published by Red Penguin Books

Bellerose Village, New York

ISBN

Print 978-1-63777-638-4 | 978-1-63777-639-1

Digital 978-1-63777-640-7

No part of this book may be reproduced in any form or by any electronic or mechanical means, including information storage and retrieval systems, without written permission from the author, except for the use of brief quotations in a book review.

*For my mother, Carmela (everyone calls her Millie). Her support and sense of humor have been with me my entire life.
There is a little bit of her and my father in every column I write.
Also, she still irons my shirts...*

CONTENTS

Introduction	xi
1. My Father is Dating a Redhead in Heaven	1
2. Holiday Hangover	5
3. New Year's Resolutions I Can Keep	9
4. The Importance of Family Traditions	13
5. An Email Plea for Assistance	17
6. The "S" Word	21
7. A Letter to 14-Year-Old Me	25
8. Getting My Driver's License	29
9. The Angel from Brooklyn	33
10. "Let's Be Careful Out There…"	37
11. 30 Years in the Blink of an Eye	41
12. A Few Hours at the DMV	45
13. The Burden of Paying It Forward	49
14. The Corona Virus Hits Home	53
15. Marry Again? Depends On Who You Ask	57
16. My Little League Nightmare Story	61
17. My Mother's Retirement Plan	65
18. The Horror of Losing Your Cell Phone	69
19. My Stupid House	73
20. Vacationing With and Without the Kids	77
21. I'm Unprepared for the Apocalypse	83
22. My Uncle Sammy the War Hero	87
23. Make Mine a Whopper	93
24. The Death of the Caped Crusader	97
25. Louie the Labrador Speaks Out	101
26. Remembering My Father	105
27. Good Grief, A Surprise Arrives in the Mail	109
28. Time to Rethink How We Celebrate Weddings?	113
29. The Loss of a Furry Friend	117
30. The Night the Lights Went Out in Brooklyn	121
31. Time to Leave the Nest and Fly Away	125
32. Understanding the Sacrifices of Our Veterans	129
33. Oh My! I Have Onychophagia	133

34. The Mystery of August 14th, 2003	137
35. Where is My Wife?	143
36. The Scourge of Long Island: The Cave Cricket	147
37. Welcome to the Family	151
38. There Is Crying in Baseball	155
39. Another Summer has Come and Gone	159
40. Where Everybody Knows Your Name	163
41. Enough Already with Pumpkin Spice	167
42. A Sandy Story	171
43. My Appliances are Plotting Against me	177
44. My Mother's Best Halloween	181
45. Trying the Impossible Whopper	185
46. Why You Should Respect the Flag	189
47. What Happened to Trick or Treating?	193
48. Celebrating Thanksgiving Italian Style	197
49. Remembering John Lennon	201
50. A Love Affair With My Snowblower	205
51. You Never Stop Being a Parent, Ever	209
52. The Magic of Santa	213
Shortcuts	217
Afterword	221
Acknowledgments	223
About the Author	227
Also by Paul DiSclafani	229

INTRODUCTION

I'd like to take you on a journey.

The stories and essays contained in this collection will take you to many different places. Most will make you laugh; others will make you think. Some will make you reflect, bringing you back to another time in your life, when the kids were little, or when things were much simpler.

Although some stories are very personal and about my immediate family, they are also about you and your family. You see, we're not all that different when you get right down to it. We grow up and get older, deal with children, aging parents, spouses, and siblings. We have jobs, debts to pay, and appliances that are plotting against us.

We have friends we don't see enough, and faults that we don't normally talk about in public. We've lost people close to us while also celebrating new family members.

But most of all, we have stories to tell.

Although some of these stories come from my own personal experiences, I try to tell them as though I was an outsider observer. Like a guy sitting on a park bench watching the world go by, you can view a lot of things unfolding in front of you from that bench, both with your eyes and your memories.

I've been fortunate enough to share my stories with the readers of the *Massapequa Observer* (part of the Anton News Group) every week since 2017 through my column called "Long Island Living." Massapequa is a town in southern Nassau County, on Long Island, in the state of New York.

I decided not to edit these stories as I wanted you to experience them as they were first published, warts and all. It also allows you, as the reader, to see how my writing style has developed (and hopefully improved) over the years.

I've added an introduction and some historical content to each column to give you a little more depth, sometimes adding a story behind the story.

For this collection, I have selected several of my favorite columns, allowing the reader to experience them as they would from a weekly columnist. Of course, you could just read the table of contents, and pick a story to be read based on title, but that would ruin the mystery of the journey. Sometimes it's better to put the map away and just keep driving forward. For those of you who prefer doing your reading in the "John" and are looking for something specific to read, I've added a section in the back of the book. It's called "Shortcuts" and organizes the stories by category, like "Something to Make You Laugh," "Conversation Starters," and "Let Me Tell You a Story…"

For the rest of you, my dear readers, I want you to enjoy them one at a time, never knowing what story will come next when you turn the page. Like Forrest Gump's mother told him, "Life is like a box of chocolates. You never know what you'll get."

Why not turn the page and see what you get?

Let me tell you a story...

MY FATHER IS DATING A REDHEAD IN HEAVEN

(2019)

My father passed away in 2010 after a long bout with a muscular disease called "Limb Girdle." My mother was his primary caregiver for most of the last ten years of his life before he required full-time nursing care in 2008. As kids, my parents lived just three houses from each other in the East New York section of Brooklyn.

My mother is also a big believer in dreams and visions. She loves to look at license plates when we drive around and point out a sequence of numbers that tells her my father is watching over us. His birthday (28) or their anniversary (26) are usually involved. Sometimes, she sees all the numbers scrambled, like 2268.

I stopped by my mother's house one afternoon to drop off my work shirts for her to iron, and she started to tell me this story. If it had been anyone else, I would have thought they were making it up. But not my mother, and especially not when it comes to dreaming about my father.

This column was submitted to the Press Club of Long Island for the 2020 Media Awards and helped me win Second Place in the "Narrative-Column" category.

And yes, before you ask, please understand that my mother loves to iron; and if I don't bring her my shirts, I get yelled at...

My Father is Dating a Redhead in Heaven
By Paul DiSclafani

My mother, who just turned 87, continues to dream vividly, in color, and remembers every detail. That's how she found out my father is dating a redhead in heaven.

"I dreamt of your father last night," she told me the other day. "He said he had something to tell me that I wasn't going to like. He fell in love with someone."

Fell in love with someone?

"How is that even possible?" I asked, not knowing you could date in heaven. "He told me he doesn't know how it happened," she continued, "but he doesn't love me anymore."

My father, who was never known as a "Hound Dog," has been dead for almost 10 years now, and, quite frankly, this came as a shock to me. After all, he began dating my mother when she was a teenager, why the sudden interest in a redheaded woman in heaven?

I asked my mother about which dad she sees in heaven, young dad or old dad? "He's 33 years old," she told me, admonishing me for not knowing the rules of heaven. "Everyone is 33 years old in heaven. That's how old Jesus was when he died."

Fascinated with where this might be going, I asked, "How do you know she was a redhead?"

"She was standing right next to him," she said.

Wow. Talk about an awkward situation. Then, she began yelling at my father. "After all those years together and how I took care of you when you were sick," she said she told him, "You turn around and do this to me?"

I was so intrigued by the sudden dramatic turn of events; I needed to know what happened next.

"Then I woke up and had to go to the bathroom," she said.

Oh, the humanity! Now I was never going to find out what happened.

Except my mother is the Queen of Dreaming. Instead of coming back to bed and changing the channel in her brain, it was just a commercial break. She fell asleep and continued participating in her personal Soap Opera, "As Heaven Turns."

"She had the nerve to tell me to leave him alone," she said of the nasty redhead, "And there was nothing I could do about it." Surely my mother wasn't going to give in to this home-wrecking hussy, right? "Then again," she said solemnly, "I'm probably not going to get into heaven."

Wait just a minute, young lady.

"You have as much of a chance at getting into heaven as anyone," I reminded her. Besides, how does a home-wrecking hussy get into heaven anyway? Have the rules been relaxed since the last time I read *The Bible*? Then again, marriage vows do stipulate, "Till death do us part." There doesn't seem to be a provision for the Afterlife.

I'm certainly not going to waste St. Peter's time in line at the Pearly Gates, but my mother? She punched her ticket there a long time ago. At some point, she will get there, and at some point, my transformed, 33-year-old mother is going to run into Miss Redhead.

I only hope that the reunion will be available as a Pay-Per-View dream that we all could see.

HOLIDAY HANGOVER

(2020)

I love the holidays as much as the next guy, but I think we all get a nasty hangover at the beginning of January every year.

There is nothing worse than waking up after a great party, only to realize that now you must clean up everything. That's what happens at some point every January.

I've always tried to be honest with my readers. In this column, I decided to say what everyone was really feeling, but no one would admit.

Holiday Hangover
By Paul DiSclafani

Come on, you can admit it.

There is nothing more joyful and heartwarming than the holiday season. It starts with Thanksgiving, fast forwards to the different religious holidays in late December, and culminates with the celebration of reflection and hope when we ring in the New Year.

For most, gathering with family and friends to share meals, good times, and gifts creates memories that last a lifetime. It's a time to reflect on those we have loved and lost, and a chance to look forward to the promise of the future.

But now it's time to say, "Thank goodness, that's over."

I don't believe I'm a Bah Humbug when saying many people are happy the holidays are over so they can go back to their regular routines. Who thought that getting up, going to work, coming home, having dinner, and going to bed at a decent hour was something to look forward to?

How is it that people who genuinely love the holidays are so sapped and drained by the time they are over? Friends and relatives who love this time of year couldn't wait to take everything down and put their house back together.

This year, Christmas and New Year's Day fell in the middle of the week, throwing most of us for a loop. When you consider that both holidays are preceded by overeating and late-night celebrations on their "Eve," that essentially gives us four holidays over eight days. When celebrating multiple holidays with a weekend in between, you can lose track of what day it is.

At my age, New Year's Day is no longer reserved for treating a hangover. It's become a day to step back, take a breath, and do nothing more than watch *The Honeymooners* marathon. Maybe we are suffering from a post-holiday depression, but it feels more like a vacation jetlag.

During the holidays, you seem to be on a perpetual vacation. You stay up late for no reason and eat way too much. You are always on the go and traveling, cramming way too many activities into a short time.

When your vacation is over, your body is exhausted and just wants to crash. That's what the first few days of January are like every year, the end of your month-long holiday vacation. Staying up late on New Year's Eve isn't what's dragging your brain through the mud the next day. It's your body finally raising the white flag to signal the end of the holidays.

We spent the better part of an entire weekend getting the inside of our house ready for Christmas. Many of you devoted an extra weekend to also decorate the outside of your home. Since most people don't have a tree in their living room the other 11 months of the year, furniture most likely needed to be relocated. Boxes of decorations and trimmings needed to be excavated from the basement or garage.

Now that the holidays are over, everything must be reversed. Empty storage containers need to be refilled and returned to their place of origin. If you have a real tree, it needs to be disposed of. If you decorated the outside of your house, I'm quite sure it is a lot colder in January than it was back in early December when you put everything up. Take a good look at the faces of your neighbors undecorating in January. The joy you saw in their faces when setting up has been replaced with, well, you get the idea.

So, be honest. You can admit it. You love and cherish spending time with your friends and family, but you're happy the holidays are over. You may not be looking forward to taking everything down and storing it away again, but you're glad it's over.

So, relax and take a deep breath. Thanksgiving is still eleven months away...

NEW YEAR'S RESOLUTIONS I CAN KEEP

2018

After my first full year as a columnist, I decided to have some fun at my own expense.

Every year we make New Year's resolutions, and every year we break them before February rolls around. I decided to list several resolutions I know I can keep. What's the sense in resolving to do something that is not in your heart?

There is satisfaction in knowing that you are maintaining your goals during the year. It is even more satisfying when you look back and marvel at your accomplishments.

And isn't feeling good about yourself what it is all about anyway?

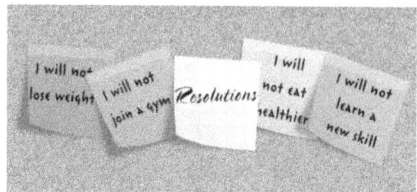

New Year's Resolutions I Can Keep
By Paul DiSclafani

What drives people to make resolutions they really do not intend to keep, just because the calendar changes from one year to another? Everyone is guilty of it at some point or on some level. For example, if you want to start watching your weight or begin to exercise, why not do it on March 29th or June 11th, or whenever you are ready? What magical powers does January 1st have?

If the start of a new calendar year helps you make "changes" in your life, more power to you. In the past, I've also used the start of a new year to help me get motivated. As you wait for the ball to drop, you reflect on the easy choices you made, like stopping at Chipotle or ordering Pizza instead of cooking.

During those final hours before the *Honeymooner's* marathon, you stare down that at the cheese dip and declare, "This is it, starting tomorrow, I'm going to make better choices," then scoop and devour as if those calories get negated come midnight. Two pieces of chocolate cake and a handful of cookies later, this year is ending on an eating binge.

Come New Year's Day, the payment for the atrocities of the previous night come due, and you are stuck with the bill. Time to reassess your lifestyle and put into play all the resolutions you declared the night before. Like most, I have promised to eat better, exercise more, and lose weight. More than 30% of people who make resolutions vow to achieve all three of these goals. Other top resolutions are "learning a new skill" and "saving money." Did you know that more than half the people who make New Year's resolutions feel they are unattainable, yet they sheepishly make them anyway?

I have learned from past disappointments of not keeping my New Year's resolutions. I know my limitations, so this year, I am making resolutions that I know I will keep. Granted, they are all things I promise NOT to do, but we are trying to be realistic, aren't we?

• **I AM NOT JOINING A GYM** – With the money I've spent over the years on gym memberships, I could be driving a BMW. I start out strong, buying into the hype and promise of a healthier lifestyle, but I fizzle out way too fast. If I were serious about exercise, I could walk Louie the Labrador or take the stairs more often. Besides, I need to lose 20 pounds before I can be seen working out in a public place.

• **I AM NOT GOING TO EAT HEALTHIER** – I will try and make better choices, but I am not going to eat healthier. Did you know the word "diet" is French for "tasteless"? Just because vegetables are healthy doesn't mean I'll begin eating Brussel sprouts or grilled asparagus. I like gluten (whatever it is) in my food. I like Carbs, but based on the number of Carbs I eat, I could probably run a marathon every day for a month. My mother always told me you can eat whatever you want in moderation. Unfortunately, if you've ever eaten at my mother's house, you pass moderation in the first 15 minutes.

• **I AM NOT GOING TO LOSE WEIGHT** – Based on the resolutions mentioned above, this one might be very attainable. I always fluctuate from week to week or month to month, but somehow the scale in January always equals the scale next December. I'm not planning on gaining weight, so isn't that a good thing?

• **I AM NOT GOING TO LEARN A NEW SKILL** – How many more skills does a 60-year-old man need to know that he hasn't already mastered? Should I take up plumbing or car repair? I have enough home improvement skills to replace outlets and light fixtures or patch damaged walls. I have already fixed leaky toilets. I am a person that can follow written directions very well. I'm a master at putting together furniture from IKEA or FURN-A-KIT. I'm not going back to school to be a doctor because, quite frankly, I can't stand the sight of blood.

For me, I know these resolutions are money in the bank. That reminds me, I'm probably not going to save any money this year, either. I wish all of you the best of luck in keeping your resolutions.

Anyone want to share a "bloomin" onion with me? That's a vegetable, right?

THE IMPORTANCE OF FAMILY TRADITIONS

2018

Family traditions around the holidays are meant to be cherished and, whenever possible, continued with every new generation. Many of my fondest memories as a kid were getting together with my cousins during Christmas.

We've tried to continue that tradition with our own family and add a few new ones of our own. As parents, we can only hope our children will continue to gather and celebrate those traditions.

In this column, I shared some of my fondest memories of my childhood, which included celebrating every Christmas Day at Grandma's house with all my cousins.

The Importance of Family Traditions
By Paul DiSclafani

Life in 2017 was certainly not like life in 1967.

In 1967, our parents were still holding on to the 1950s and just weren't ready to make the jump to light speed and into the future. Holidays were always reserved for family, but the '60s were a time of change, and, for the first time, geography was getting in the way of family gatherings.

During the Great Eastern migration to Long Island in the late '60s, many of our parents became separated from their parents for the first time by more than just a couple of blocks. Previously, the question of where you were spending Thanksgiving and Christmas never even came up—you were going to Grandma's house. If you were lucky enough to have two sets of grandparents still alive, you either split the holidays or made two visits on the same day.

It's rare today that a single family has more than just two or three children, but back then, it was common to have five or six. My mother and father had six siblings each, so that's a lot of aunts, uncles, and cousins. We didn't have a lot of friends because we didn't need them, we had cousins. Lots of them.

Thanksgiving and Christmas celebrations in Italian households are legendary, and our family was no different. The coordination of resources in the tiny kitchen area required military precision. We were barely tall enough to see over the top of the counter, but when we would venture out into the workspace, there were wooden spoons, aprons, and bee-hive hairdos as far as the eye could see. Every one of my aunts had a specific job, while every one of my uncles was upstairs taking a pre-meal nap in preparation for their post-meal nap.

As kids, our biggest gripe was having to leave the plethora of toys we got from Santa under our tree when it was time to go out. Our mothers all had the same rule—pick one toy to take with you and nothing with a lot of pieces. There was really no need to bring any new toys with you since you were about to reap a new bonanza from your aunts and uncles.

All my cousins showed up with a different toy, and once we got there, we couldn't wait to start playing with them. Sal had the Great Garloo, and I brought my new GI Joe. The girls brought girly things the boys would make fun of, but in the end, everyone fought over that inedible cupcake from the Easy-Bake Oven. My Aunt Maria, who was only three years older than all the cousins, always had the newest Beatles record. With no parents within sight, we would gather in the back room, immersing ourselves in our own make-believe world.

Rummaging through old clothes and accessories we found in a

storage closet, we invented and performed in "The Funny Show," creating ridiculous characters that would tell jokes and get into outlandish situations. Sometimes we would make believe we were The Beatles or The Monkees and perform their hit records. Everyone would play a part, and the show wouldn't end until it was time for dinner. There were no rules; we just entertained ourselves with whatever we could find back there.

As we grew and began to have families of our own, our holiday landing spots shifted to our own parents and with our own siblings. My brother and I have been lucky enough to split the Christmas holidays as both of our spouses celebrated Christmas Eve with their families. That allowed us to maintain our Christmas Day tradition with our parents, providing our children with traditions involving both sets of grandparents.

New rituals now include exchanging gifts with one set of cousins on Christmas Eve, followed by a big Christmas dinner the next day that had more gifts with another group of cousins on Christmas Day.

As we head into a new year, we mourn those we have lost, but we are thankful for those still here. Family traditions for Christmas and holidays are the most important things you can impart to your children. The lyrics from the Christmas favorite "Have Yourself a Merry Little Christmas" remind us: "Through the years we all will be together, if the fates allow…"

May the fates allow you and your families to enjoy many, many holidays together as you begin or continue traditions that provide your family with memories that will last a lifetime.

AN EMAIL PLEA FOR ASSISTANCE

2018

Like most of you, I get many emails during the year from people trying to relieve me of my money in return for even more money. Some are highly creative, others not so much. But despite all the bad grammar, misspellings, and ridiculous circumstances, they just keep coming.

I decided to detail an email plea for assistance I received in this column from 2018. This particular plea for assistance was so incredibly detailed that I thought the backstory would have made a great book. After reading it several times, I was almost convinced that I might actually be able to help my new friend, Abbah.

I had such a good time with the concept; I've carefully chosen a new scam email to respond to every year since. But as they say, you always remember your first.

An Email Plea for Assistance
By Paul DiSclafani

Since becoming a columnist for the *Massapequa Observer* in 2017, I've received some very complimentary emails from loyal readers who have enjoyed my weekly thoughts and musings. But, I recently received a desperate email from a reader that really needs my help to preserve his family's inheritance.

Abbah Abacha is a loyal online reader from the African country of Nigeria who is in a terrible situation back home. His father, the late General Sani Abacha, recently passed away, and his eldest brother, Muhammad, is being detained by Order of the Federal Government of Nigeria. What makes matters worse, his father left behind $33 million deposited in a Holland security company, and the government—the same government that is detaining Muhammad—is trying to steal the money!

How can a mild-mannered, local columnist like me help out Abbah and his family reclaim their fortune, you ask? It's quite simple, actually. They just want to transfer the $33 million into my bank account so that the corrupt Nigerian government can't get their hands on it.

The Abacha family amassed this fortune through years of hard work and shrewd business deals. Now, due to the untimely passing of the General, the Government is looking to steal it from the family and use it to fund their crooked regime. Turns out, the only way for his family to protect the money is to get it out of the country and away from the reach of the corrupt Government officials. That's where yours truly comes in.

Once the entire family fortune has been transferred out of the country and into the United States, they will create a secret bank account, and the money can then be transferred back. Easy-peasy, right? For my trouble, they will pay me handsomely for the temporary use of my bank account, allowing me to keep a percentage before transferring it back.

Now, before you get all high and mighty and think that this whole idea is crazy, hear me out first. It's not like they are trying to rip me off or asking me for money. The way I see it, they are taking all the risk. How do they know that I will hold up my end of the bargain and transfer it back?

Besides being a loyal reader of this column, Abbah trusts me implicitly. His family has suffered great trauma, humility, and deprivation since the death of his father, and he needs my help. Abbah wrote that he chose me because "an influential government functionary" gave him my name and assured him of my transparency. I assumed he meant trustworthiness, not my ability to be invisible, but sometimes the English language is difficult for foreigners to master. Of course, I'm not sure I know any influential government functionaries, but with an impassioned endorsement like that, how could I turn him down?

Judging by the tone of his email, there is a great urgency for Abbah to get this done. Choosing to use ALL CAPS, he wrote, "THE URGENCY THIS OFFER DESIRES SHALL BE TREETED WITH ALL PROMPTNESS AS ANY DAY THAT PASSES BY POSSES A BIGGER TREAT. YOU MUST UNDERSTANDE THAT THIS TRANSACTION SHOULD BE TREATED WITH ALL SECRECY, AS IT WILL AMOUNT TO CONIVIANCE IF CONFIDENTIALITY IS NOT MAINTAINED."

Aren't you glad you live in a country that has spell check?

Once I contact Abbah via email, he will send a representative out to the Security Company in Holland to assist me in completing the transaction. What could be more secure than that?

I'm a little concerned that bank accounts in this country are only insured by the FDIC for $250,000, and I'm not sure what will happen after $33 million is deposited into my account. However, I'm sure I can work something out with the IRS, considering I am helping a very wealthy foreign entity.

Oh wait, I have a joint bank account with my wife. I'm sure I'm going to need her signature when I transfer the money back. Maybe I better let her in on this before I reply to Abbah.

After all, what could possibly go wrong?

THE "S" WORD

2017

I love when my birthday comes around. I always wished my birthday was in the summer, so I could have a great big party outdoors. Alas, my birthday falls at the end of the worst month to plan a party, February 24th.

Although that has never been an impediment to me having birthday parties, they are just confined to indoor activities. I always loved the gathering of my family and friends and, of course, the presents. I have told my kids that their birthday is special, and they get a full 24 hours to enjoy it. It's weird, but I still get a kick out of seeing a digital clock showing 2:24.

But as my 60th birthday approached, I actually didn't know what to think of it. I knew it was a milestone birthday, but that didn't make me feel any better. To me, 60 was just plain old.

I decided to talk about it with my readers. It was the first time I had ever written anything that was about me personally. I was sharing my feelings with strangers for the first time. This was only the third column I had ever written, and I was just beginning to get my feet wet. My first two columns were about life in Massapequa. After submitting those columns, they were published a few weeks apart.

After I wrote this column, which they published the week I submitted it, my editor called me when I failed to send them another column. He wanted to know if I could give them something for the next edition.

The reaction from this column led me to believe that writing about events in my life might be interesting to readers. It changed everything for me as a columnist.

The "S" Word
By Paul DiSclafani

I'm going to be 60-years-old this month.

There, I said it. And don't give me that "60 is the new 50" line. It's not. It's still 60.

It has taken me a good, long time to come to grips with it, but it turns out "60" is a lot more difficult to say than I thought it was. Of course, it's just a number. To be honest, I never thought I would get this far.

When you're in your 20s, your parents are in their 50s. You can't even imagine 50 at that point, but 60? Fugheddaboutit.

Many years ago, my Uncle Paulie was turning 60. At his birthday party, I grabbed him and, in a playful way, told him, "Now you are officially old." But when he turned 70 in 2014, and I was now approaching 60, I made sure to apologize for that remark, insisting that 60 is not really "old."

I guess I wear it well because most people I encounter that don't know me are quite surprised when they find out my actual age. But I was having trouble coming to grips with actually saying "60." It just doesn't feel right saying the "S" word.

Turning 30 is a major milestone in life. That is kind of when you need to begin acting like a grown-up, and you start having responsibilities.

Turning 40 is more like a whirlwind because life is coming at you in all directions. You are most likely married, and now you are responsible not only for yourself but you may have children. Raising young children is like waking up with your hair on fire every day. And now you add in a mortgage and a Labrador retriever, and your 40s might be the most stressful period of your adult life.

Turning 50 is when you get to take a deep breath and celebrate surviving your 40s. Your kids are grown and no longer need to be micromanaged. You are (hopefully) making more money, and for the first time since the kids were born, you can almost see the light at the end of the tunnel. You can at least see the tunnel. But in your 50s, you can still be cool. Nobody looks at you any differently if you say you are 55 than they did if you were 45.

But use the "S" word, and everything changes. Some people are shocked; others seem to have empathy for you. They look at you like you lost a pet. No one is excited for you like they were when you were turning 50.

Let's face it–it's all downhill from here. I've already started losing patience with stupid things that never would have bothered me 10 years ago. Talk about being on the back-nine of life. What's left now? Finally, getting that senior discount? Becoming a grandparent? Retirement and collecting a pension for doing nothing? Playing more golf? Traveling anytime and anywhere we want? No more alarm clocks? Wearing sweatpants? Smoking more cigars?

Hey, wait a minute, that doesn't sound so bad, does it? So yeah, I'm going to be 60 in February. There, I said it, and I'm OK with that.

Now get off my lawn, you young whippersnappers.

A LETTER TO 14-YEAR-OLD ME

2018

I read an article in <u>The Athletic</u> written by Mike Bossy, the former New York Islanders star. Bossy was turning 50 and wondered what he would have told his younger self to help prepare him for the future.

It was beautifully written and made me think about what I might want to tell myself at 14. But unlike Bossy, who essentially told his younger self about his future, I wanted to go in a different direction.

I knew that the 14-year-old me had his whole life ahead of him and, at that age, wasn't too concerned about the future. I didn't want to give myself too much of a glimpse into the future because I didn't want to ruin the movie, as I said in the column.

There's a funny line at the end that is a little out of context. It refers to an embarrassing event at a Little League game. It references a previously published column from 2017, "My Little League Nightmare Story."

That column is also part of this collection.

A Letter to a 14-year-old Me
By Paul DiSclafani

Dear 14-Year-Old Paul:

First, I hope you had a great birthday last weekend. Actually, it was our birthday. You see, I am writing to you today as the 60-year-old man you grew up to be. This letter is coming from the future, your future. Our future.

It's 1971, and you are almost done with Junior High School, which they now call Middle School here on Long Island. High School may seem a little daunting because the Seniors are so big, but you know that growth spurt Mom and Dad have been telling you about? It never actually comes for you. Don't get me wrong, you still grow to be a healthy adult, but you're not going to make the basketball team.

Now that you know a little about being a teenager, try and enjoy the next few years. High School is really different from Junior High, and the work is much more challenging. Your social life becomes front and center, but not everyone needs to like you, and not everyone wants to be your friend. That's just the way it goes, and that's OK. Dr. Seuss said, "Those who mind don't matter, and those that matter don't mind."

You know how much you like baseball, especially the Mets? You will have a lot of ups and downs with that team, my friend, but stick with it and stay true to the Orange and Blue. They will break your heart a lot, but what are you going to do, root for the Yankees?

By the way, I know that girls are starting to make their way into your little group of friends, but they are nothing but trouble at this point. You think the Mets are going to break your heart? Sports may not be an excellent substitute for girls, but it is a pretty good alternative. And just so you know, nobody is making out with girls as much as they say they are.

Girlfriends will come and go, only don't get your hopes up for setting any records. Unfortunately, you are a reasonably shy kid and worry way too much about getting rejected. At some point, you find the girl of your dreams, and you will just know that she's the one. To this day, I can't explain it, you just know.

Don't hesitate to take that journalism class in 11th grade; it will change your life. It will begin your journey with the written word. You will work on the school radio station and when you get to college, believe it or not, you will be the sports editor for two different schools. But before you get too excited, real jobs in journalism are few and far between in the '80s. Hang in there with computers; that's the future.

Turns out you have a pretty good sense of humor, so learn to use it wisely. You also are a pretty good organizer, so just remember if you don't get those tickets for everyone, your entire group will never go anywhere. Before you know it, you'll begin taking driving lessons and getting your license. You are going to get a really crappy car to start out with and after just 48 hours, let's just say you will be glad it was a crappy car.

You are really going to enjoy your 20's. During those carefree days, you will make friends for life and go to concerts, finding out about a singer named Bruce Springsteen. Hold onto the people in your life that are always there for you. Don't waste time worrying about those that walk away; it's not worth it.

Trust in destiny, my young friend, and you'll never fret over making the wrong decision. Whatever decision you make works out just fine. Don't sweat the past, keep living in the present, and look forward to the future. Have confidence in yourself because you have a lot figured out, more than you realize. Take that chance. You never want to say, "I should have."

This journey we call life has a lot of ups and downs. You are going to laugh a lot, cry a little, and have an excellent time along the way. Just remember, your family is everything. Hang out with your little brother more often and include him in your life. When you guys get older, you will realize he is as cool as you.

Follow your heart and always listen to the little man in your head. I won't tell you specifics of the future because I don't want to ruin the movie for you. Just believe me when I say it's really a fun ride. By the way, hang in there with that new hockey team, the New York Islanders; it gets much better in a few years.

Alright, maybe just one specific thing.

This spring, when you get that single in Little League with all your cousins watching, stay on the base. The first baseman still has the ball…

GETTING MY DRIVER'S LICENSE

2019

This is one of the first milestones a kid reaches (after becoming a teenager). It meant true independence. Of course, having a license without access to a car would have been frustrating.

Before my road test, I bought a car from my Aunt Maria (who was only three years older than me) for $200 in 1974. It was a red 1962 Plymouth Valiant convertible. Unfortunately, the convertible roof didn't go up and down automatically anymore. Still, with a little coercion and some help from your friends, you could make it work.

Most of my friends were a year older than me and already had their licenses and, in some cases, their own car. I couldn't wait to be behind the wheel and on my own. More importantly, I would have my license before my Senior year began.

Every word of this story is true.

Getting My Driver's License
By Paul DiSclafani

Hard to believe, but I'm coming up on 45 years of driving.

Full disclosure, I failed my permit test. Can you believe that? I read the handbook, went in with a massive chip on my shoulder, and bombed. Talk about humiliation. There's not a huge stigma in failing your road test, but the permit test? Two weeks later, after studying that stupid book day and night, I scored 20 out of 20.

Being born in February, I was eligible for Driver's Ed in the summer of 1974, between my Junior and Senior year. That meant I would have my license by early August, plenty of time to cruise the rest of the summer before school started. To make sure, I scheduled my road test weeks in advance, coinciding with the end of summer classes.

My father and I practiced merging on and off parkway ramps and going out into the intersection when making a left at a light, something many people don't do anymore. "Rainman" had nothing on me; I was an excellent driver. Not to brag, but I could also execute a mean parallel park.

When the big day came, I was ready. Comfortably belted in our family's 1964 Buick Skylark, the examiner directed me to pull away from the curb, and off we went. After performing a magnificent left turn at the corner, he pointed to a parked car asking me to execute a parallel park. A sly smile came across my face, knowing it was showtime! I pulled even with the parked vehicle and began my backward maneuver, slowly angling behind the car, then straightening out in a sequence of events that was so beautifully choreographed, I was expecting him to stop the test right there and give me a standing ovation.

Then I bumped into the car behind me.

There was a car behind me? The examiner seemed as startled as I was. After all, I only practiced this with a single vehicle, never parking between two cars. I don't even remember noticing that car. Three minutes into my road test, I had failed on the one maneuver I thought I had mastered. The examiner just calmly said, "Pull out and continue down the block." I was mortified and completely bummed. With nothing to lose at this point, I indignantly slapped the driveshaft out of Park, snapped on the blinker, shoved my hand out the window, and continued. I still had to do a K-turn, make a few other maneuvers, and my torture would be over.

It was a long, quiet ride home with my father. We discussed rescheduling another test, but they were booked until September, meaning I wouldn't have my license until after school started. Of course, the tale I told my friends made me sound like a badass, telling off the examiner for making me park between two vehicles. Anything to soften the blow of the rejection letter I'd get in the coming days, instead of my temporary license.

When the letter arrived in the mail on a Friday, I didn't even want to open it. But instead of getting a "Dear John" letter, it was my temporary license! How was that possible? I believe that was the moment I invented the "Happy Dance."

Later that wonderful August evening, my friends and I piled into my red, 1962 Plymouth Valiant I bought a few weeks earlier for $200. It had a push-button transmission and a convertible roof that didn't go down into the trunk unless you jumped up and down on it.

As we cruised Merrick Road like Royalty, someone shouted, "Look at the chicks at that place!" We all turned in unison to check out the bevy of beauties. Unfortunately, the car in front of me decided to stop and make a left turn.

Need I say more?

My fantasy of cruising the streets of Long Island in a convertible as the summer of '74 wound down was dashed. Apparently, there weren't a lot of radiators for a 1962 Plymouth Valiant available at junkyards.

It's been 45 years, and I still cringe every time I pass that intersection.

THE ANGEL FROM BROOKLYN

2020

Every now and then, events happen that make you wonder if there really is a supreme being, or at least a Guardian Angel, looking out for you or your loved ones.

This story certainly puts that theory to the test. It's about a chance meeting at a gas station between an elderly woman (my mother) and a Good Samaritan stranger. It just so happens that he hailed from her old neighborhood in East New York.

Then again, maybe some people are just good-natured.

This column helped "Long Island Living" win First Place for the category "Narrative-Column" in the 2021 Press Club of Long Island Media Awards.

The Angel from Brooklyn
By Paul DiSclafani

My mother didn't get her driver's license until she was about 40 years old. As a typical 1950's mom, she stayed home to take care of the children, the house, and nearly everything that didn't involve earning money. After the great migration to Long Island in the late '60s, most Brooklynites were now saddled with a mortgage. With my brother and me in school all day, my mother joined the workforce to help make ends meet.

After working locally down the block at Mays Department store, she took another job a few miles away (in Lindenhurst) that required transportation. She carpooled with a friend for a few months as a passenger, eventually making the decision to call a local driving instructor from down the block. There was no possible way my father was going to teach her how to drive. They would be divorced in less than three lessons.

My mother never learned how to ride a bicycle, yet she wanted to pilot a 2,000-pound vehicle. Her sense of direction was always a question mark, once getting lost just walking around our block. But she'd figured out how to get from Point A to Point B with two particular caveats; she doesn't drive on parkways, and she doesn't pump her own gas.

For 47 years, she has always found a station to pump her gas. Please understand that my mother needs gas about as often as a camel needs water. She has a 2013 Honda Civic with 7,000 miles on it. Most people log more than 1,000 miles a month, not a year.

Many gas stations used to offer "full" service, but unless you live in New Jersey, where all the stations pump gas for you, locating that today is as difficult as finding a payphone. I'll occasionally take her car and fill it (that lasts about three months), but sometimes she relies on strangers.

Recently, she stopped at a station on Merrick Road, where she had previous success with the clerk pumping the gas for her. She saw a man coming out and asked if he worked there. He had a kind face and told her that he had just gone in for a cup of coffee but asked if she needed help with something. Explaining her dilemma, he gladly offered to pump the gas for her.

She gave him $20 and asked if he could get $10 worth of gas for her.

"How do you know I won't just take your money?" he said with a sly smile on his face.

"I trust you," she said.

With that, he returned, handed her back the $10 change, asked if she would hold his coffee, then started pumping her gas.

Striking up a conversation, my mother was very appreciative and asked his name and where he was from.

"My name is Michael," he offered, "And I lived in the East New York section of Brooklyn for most of my life."

My mother is also from East New York, and it turns out they lived not too far from each other and knew a lot of the familiar landmarks.

While reminiscing together, she mentioned her grandson was also named Michael. He responded that he also had a son named Michael, and he was a police officer in Nassau County. What are the odds? Her Michael (my nephew) is also a Nassau County Police Officer!

She offered him a dollar for his time (he declined, of course), handed him back his coffee, and they went their separate ways. In the five minutes it took to put $10 gas into her car (a little more than three gallons at today's prices), my mother was convinced that this Michael was an Angel sent from heaven to help in her time of need.

Who knows, maybe he was…

"LET'S BE CAREFUL OUT THERE..."

2018

I had attended the Swearing-In Ceremony for the 2018 Nassau County Police Department. I was taken aback by the number of new officers, which included my nephew Michael. They were swearing an oath to protect the citizens of Nassau County.

My wife is a retired NYPD Sergeant. There wasn't a day that went by without me thinking about her out on the streets.

Now, this new crop of police officers would be taking their first step in what many hoped would become a long career in law enforcement. Every one of them is aware of the danger, yet this is their chosen profession. That makes them special.

I wanted them all to know that I understood what they were swearing an oath to undertake.

"Let's Be Careful Out There..."
By Paul DiSclafani

For most of the 1980s, a popular police drama, *Hill Street Blues*, dominated the Nielson ratings. The show was set in a fictional police precinct in a fictional town but dealt with real-life situations faced by police officers every day. The audience was drawn to the characters, some of whom may have been a little too cartoonish, but it's all entertainment, right?

Every episode began the same way, with the rank-and-file officers gathering in the squad room during roll call as they prepared to head onto the streets to serve and protect the citizens. The daily briefing updated the officers' shift of what was going on and what they should be looking out for during their upcoming tour. This was standard practice in every police precinct in America. Some officers would be joking around and not paying attention while the Sergeant reviewed the more mundane items. But just before they were released, Sergeant Phil Esterhaus (played by actor Michael Conrad) would give them one last command, pointing his finger at them and saying, "Let's be careful out there."

That's all I could think of when I attended the graduation ceremony of the more than 160 graduates of the Nassau County police department on February 8th at Hofstra. These recruits have chosen a profession that puts them directly in harm's way, swearing an oath to "serve and protect" the 1.3 million residents of Nassau County. This batch of peacekeepers ranged in all shapes and sizes, all races and creeds, all religions. Each of them was perfectly coiffed with their shiny shoes and matching blue uniforms and ties. They responded with military-like precision as they proudly received their graduation certificates from the new Nassau County Executive, Laura Curran, and the new Police Commissioner, Patrick Ryder.

With the stands packed with proud parents, siblings, relatives, and friends, each of them paused for a picture with the dignitaries as they cherished this moment, a culmination of hard work and determination. A moment frozen in time. A moment that chronicles the beginning of their life-long journey into law enforcement, in a calling that is reserved for a brotherhood of a few proud and dedicated individuals.

And my nephew Michael is now one of them.

This graduating class included the men and women who would become not only Nassau County Police Officers but serve private town forces, like Glen Cove, Freeport, Hempstead, and Garden City. It included Sheriff's Deputies and Medics. All of them had to pass a grueling seven-month training that involved physical fitness, defensive tactics, firearm usage, and education. Not every recruit made it through the rigorous training, but those who did could be proud of their accomplishments.

Before the recruits were called upon to receive their certifications, many law enforcement members spoke at length while congratulating them for their perseverance and desire to be a police officer and cautioning them about the dangers of the job. There wasn't a person in that Hofstra auditorium that didn't know of the dangers of being a police officer, especially in today's world.

But this celebration was about the achievements of this graduating class who will begin their new careers the next day. We can be assured that they have been trained and, more importantly, prepared to take to the streets to protect us all the time.

As the recruits advanced to the stage in a single file of perfectly pressed shirts and pants, they waited patiently for their name to be announced. As their friends and family cheered for them, you couldn't help but think of how they all got there. Many have been preparing for this moment all their lives, following in a relative's footprints or just chasing a dream. As kids, everyone played cops and robbers, arresting the bad guys and saving the day. They were Batman and Spiderman, Wonder Woman or Princess Leia.

It seemed like just yesterday that Michael was up on a different stage, being lauded for achieving Eagle Scout's rank and talking about a possible career in law enforcement. Now his dream, along with those of all the recruits, has finally become a reality. After all those years of pretending to be Superheroes, today they indeed are heroes.

Let's be careful out there…

30 YEARS IN THE BLINK OF AN EYE

2019

This column was written when my first-born son, James, turned 30-years old. His girlfriend, Ellyn, organized a surprise birthday party for him and his friends at the Post Office Café in Babylon on Long Island.

James has been friends with most of these kids since they played baseball together in Little League. Later, as young adults, I was their coach for most of those years. I've watched them grow up from kids, to gangly teenagers, to full-fledged adults. They still call me "coach" when I see them.

This column is one of those that came from the heart. If you have grown children, you can understand where my head was when I wrote this one. Every time I read it, it makes me a little weepy.

This column was submitted to the Press Club of Long Island for their 2020 Media Awards and helped me win Second Place in the "Narrative-Column" category.

30 Years in the Blink of an Eye
By Paul DiSclafani

While waiting at the Post Office Café for the Guest of Honor, I observed the collection of friends and family milling around and smiled. I've known most of them since they were kids, and here they were, all grown up, having drinks and cracking jokes while waiting for my son James to arrive at his surprise 30th Birthday party.

I can't believe I have a 30-year-old son. To be honest, that was a lot harder to say than I thought. Of course, many people my age have already gone through the "My Kid Is Turning 30" phase of their life, so be gentle with me.

How did 30 years go by so quickly? Wasn't he just a kid swinging a wiffle-ball bat in the backyard? How long ago was it that I was his hero? Weren't we just laughing hysterically at me doing something silly in McDonald's with French fries? When he didn't make the school baseball team, I might have cried more than he did.

Although he may not have known it at the time, leaving him alone at a college dorm for the first time was a very emotional experience for us. You just don't stop being a parent because your child's physical body isn't under your roof anymore. Go ask your 80-year-old mother that question and see what she tells you.

Like every set of parents, our lives were changed on the night he was born. We did all the prep work, even visiting the hospital (Mid-Island in Bethpage) for a "walk through." We learned where to park, what entrance to go through, what desk to report to, and other logistics. When the big event happened, we would be prepared.

But as we all know, Humans plan and God laughs. Things started to get real about three in the morning as my wife spoke incoherently to her obstetrician during contractions. When I took the phone, he told me in a very calm voice, "Take her to Good Samaritan Hospital right now."

Did he say right now?

That wasn't the plan. We practiced and knew every inch of Mid-Island's maternity ward. Again, in a very calm voice, he told me to take her to Good Sam right now as he had a C-Section scheduled there at 9:00 a.m., and our baby was going to be born soon.

Grabbing my wife and our "Go-Bag," we raced down to Montauk Highway for the 10-mile trek to Good Sam. Montauk Highway is a rural route filled with traffic lights so naturally, I was looking forward to taking advantage of my "situation." After all, it was very early in the morning, no one was really on the road, and there were so many red lights in front of me. So, I did what every first-time father would do with a moaning, pregnant wife in his front seat-I blew every red light and bent the speed limit where I safely could. I was secretly hoping to get pulled over, explain my situation, and enjoy a police escort. Then again, where's a police car when you really need them?

When he was born about an hour or so later, I got to hold him in my arms for the first time and, well, need I say more? It was now our job to take care of him, teach him how to be a decent, loving human being, pick him up when he was down and prepare him for this journey we call life. I'd like to think we've done that, knock on wood.

And in the blink of an eye, he reaches the first true milestone of adulthood. Celebrating the event with his friends and watching them still interacting and enjoying each other's company like they were teenagers was heartwarming. They are all growing into adults and enjoying every minute of it, just like we did.

In my eyes, he'll always be that 12-year-old kid in the backyard, playing wiffle ball with those same friends, daring me to strike them out. Which I did, just about every time. Wish I could turn back time and relive those moments.

Then again, don't we all?

A FEW HOURS AT THE DMV

2020

Sometimes I just want to write something silly. This was one of those times.

I had to renew my driver's license, and, to get the new "Real ID" license, you must visit the DMV. I made the trek and had to spend a few hours inside, waiting for my assigned number to be called.

This was just a few weeks pre-pandemic. However, there was a glut of people trying to get licenses and identification due to New York State allowing undocumented aliens to get an ID beginning on January 1, 2020. The local DMV offices were so overloaded that they enacted an optional "reservation" system to alleviate the long lines.

My license was going to expire on my birthday, so I needed to get it done quickly. I had driven past the Massapequa DMV several times in the early morning, only to see many people waiting outside the building to get inside. I thought it might be better to go in the late afternoon.

I decided to present the story to the reader in a time-line format to experience what I was experiencing. It reminded me of watching an episode of <u>Dragnet</u>. As it turned out, this was one of my most popular columns in 2020.

This column took home Second Place in the 2021 Press Club of Long Island Media Awards for "Humor Column."

. . .

A Few Hours at the DMV
By Paul DiSclafani

After hearing the horror stories on the news about the long lines at the DMV recently, I decided to give it a try in the late afternoon. To get a Real ID license, I needed to make an in-person visit, so I went to the DMV in Massapequa. The story you are about to read is mostly true. The names have been changed to protect the innocent.

3:51 p.m.

The parking lot is full, but there doesn't seem to be a line coming out of the DMV office located on the inside corner of the "L" shaped building. It looks like I made the right decision.

3:56 p.m.

The greeter directed me to two lines in front of the photo station. I chose the one on the left with four people instead of the one with six.

4:02 p.m.

My line is not moving. I got the greeter's attention with the universal "What's going on?" signal, holding my palms up. "That's not a line," he shouted. "That's just some people standing around." I silently moved to the real line, which now had eight people in front of me.

4:13 p.m.

The pleasant clerk took my photo and asked to review my paperwork. "This isn't half bad," I thought. She typed a few keystrokes into the computer and said, "Everything looks good, sir," handing it all back to me with a little piece of paper with the number U803 on it, requesting I take a seat. Bummer. I sat in the front near the counters, and waited for U803 to be called.

4:32 p.m.

Hearing the robotic voice making announcements every time a new number was called, I wanted to yell out "BINGO" just for laughs. Casually, I smiled at the person next to me, asking how long he had been waiting. He said since last Tuesday. He wasn't laughing…

A FEW HOURS AT THE DMV | 47

5:11 p.m.

The woman directly in front of me working at counter 7 has been dawdling for more than 10 minutes without calling a number. The staff at counters 6 and 8 are processing a lot of customers while 7 is still trying to get comfortable in her chair. Finally, she calls the number "R514."

5:23 p.m.

Starting to wonder if I will ever see my wife and children again. I just want one last chance to say goodbye.

5:41 p.m.

Things are deteriorating rapidly. There hasn't been a "Q" or "U" number called in more than 20 minutes. Someone drew a picture of the woman at counter 7 on form MV-44 and burned it in protest. She processed just two numbers in the last half hour. The woman at counter 8 is suddenly moving much faster.

5:49 p.m.

A shirtless man with his necktie wrapped around his forehead like a bandana is running up and down the aisles shouting, "What happened to the Q's?"

6:00 p.m.

Counter 7 has gone dark. The woman is missing. The workers at counters 6 and 8 are wearing black armbands, and I believe there was a moment of silence.

6:17 p.m.

Spied a woman in the row next to me waiting for "U801" to be called. We bonded and vowed to marry if we ever got out of here alive.

6:42 p.m.

Starting to lose consciousness. Wait, did I just hear "U801?" I turned to congratulate my new friend, but she was gone. Godspeed "U801," Godspeed...

6:57 p.m.

I slipped from my chair when my number appeared on the board, dropping to my knees to thank our creator. Making my way to counter 10 with tears in my eyes, I presented my paperwork. I turned to view those still waiting their turn and felt pity for them. Then I heard the customer at counter 11 say, "What do you mean you can't complete the transaction?"

7:58 p.m.

I woke up in the ambulance with my wife holding my hand. She told me for the last 20 minutes, I just kept babbling, "The system is down; the system is down…"

THE BURDEN OF PAYING IT FORWARD

2018

This is another in a long line of true stories; only this one happened to me.

You all know the concept of "paying it forward" by now. A stranger does a good deed for you, and you do a good deed for another stranger. In theory, you are making the world a better place with random acts of kindness.

Except it doesn't always work that way.

The world is a dangerous place sometimes. The days of stopping to assist a damsel in distress because it's the right thing to do are behind us. Now you have to worry about two thugs hiding in the woods behind her to mug you and take your car. You just never know. Unless you wear a cape and leotards, it might be better to use your cell phone and call 911.

But when you receive much-needed assistance from a stranger, there is no greater feeling for your knight in shining armor.

That's what happened to me in the days before everyone had a cell phone when my car broke down on the Northern State Parkway. My Good Samaritan not only had a car phone (it looked like something out of a James Bond movie), but he didn't want any money after allowing me to use it.

He only wanted one thing...

The Burden of Paying It Forward
By Paul DiSclafani

I was driving home from work on the Northern State Parkway in the early '90s when the drive-train on my Honda snapped. I heard it "Ka-Chunk" and immediately began losing acceleration. I maneuvered to the right lane and onto the grassy knoll somewhere between Lakeville Road and New Hyde Park Road, rolling to a halt. Now what?

Darkness was approaching, and although my membership in the Allstate Motor Club included free towing, it would be another few years before I got my first cell phone. I recalled that Driver's Ed taught us to open the hood and trunk to signal the vehicle was disabled. Surely someone would stop and offer me some help, right?

But no one stopped. As my fellow commuters continued their crawl home, I thought about how I might be identified on the "Shadow Traffic" reports by now as a "disabled vehicle on the Northern State Parkway causing rubbernecking." Just then, a guy in a cool looking sports car pulled over and offered to help.

He asked if I wanted to make a phone call and reached for a handset connected by a wire in between the two seats. I had only seen car phones in the movies, so I looked at him with adoring eyes and asked if he was James Bond?

I made my calls and shook his hand, ever so grateful for his help. I dug into my pocket to reimburse him for the calls, but he shook his head and replied, "Just help someone else out in the future when you can."

For the rest of the evening, I couldn't get James Bond out of my mind. It wasn't the cool car you could make calls from or that he took the time to stop and help. It was what he said, "Just help someone else out in the future when you can." That was a tremendous responsibility to place on someone's head, don't you think? Couldn't I have just given him $10 and called it a day? Had someone helped him once, and now he was just passing it on to me to keep the chain going? In today's vernacular, it's called "Paying it forward."

For a while, every time I passed a disabled motorist, I felt guilty for not stopping and helping them. The burden of my "Pay it forward" pact with James Bond was beginning to wear on me. With all the horror stories about people setting traps for Good Samaritans, I hesitated to make myself a victim. But then again, if not for Mr. Bond, how long would I have been out there?

It was Christmas time at a packed Sunrise Mall years later when a young kid and his girlfriend approached me in the parking lot, seeking jumper cables to help start his car. Immediately, a sly smile crossed my lips, and I knew this was it; this was my chance to unburden myself! The thought of helping this poor kid was almost secondary to me. It was a public place, it was broad daylight, and there was no danger of this being a scam.

I quickly agreed and could tell how relieved he was. As his car roared back to life, I could feel the weight being lifted off my shoulders. I had fulfilled my promise to James Bond all those years ago. Now, I could continue to pass by stranded motorists with impunity!

The kid got out of his car and reached out to shake my hand, grateful for my help, and offered to reward me for my benevolence. Before the words could escape from my mouth, I paused and thought about what I was about to lay on his head. Did I really want to burden this kid with a life-long vow? Calmly, I shook my head and turned down his offer before getting back into my car. I knew I had done the right thing and finally paid my debt forward after all those years.

As I drove past them, I rolled down my window and wished them a Merry Christmas. And just for fun, I said, "Just make sure you help someone else out in the future when you can." Without understanding what he was about to commit to, he looked at me and said, "Sure thing, mister."

To this day, I wonder if that kid ever lived up to his end of the bargain, or has he been cursing me ever since…

THE CORONA VIRUS HITS HOME

2020

This column was submitted to the Press Club of Long Island and helped me win Second Place in the "Narrative-Column" category in 2020.

Many families experienced loss due to the Corona Virus and my family was no different. We lost my mother's brother, my Uncle Anthony, on April 16th, 2020.

What was frustrating was our inability to grieve properly as a family.

My uncle spent a few weeks in the hospital as the virus slowly took his life without any of us able to visit him. When he finally succumbed to the virus, we were left to grieve alone.

Like most of you, we read about it in the paper and saw it on the news every day. But it's not until it comes right up to you and slaps you in the face that you realize how terrible this thing really was.

For our family, it hit home on April 16th…

The Corona Virus Hits Home
By Paul DiSclafani

There is no escaping the numbers every day. It doesn't matter what news channel you watch or what you read in your favorite newspaper. We are being bombarded with COVID-19 statistics.

Numbers identifying new cases are added daily to an ever-increasing total. *Newsday* is providing the total number of infected residents for every town in both Nassau and Suffolk counties.

Then, there are the numbers of people dying from the virus. The numbers vary from day-to-day with staggering results as New York State is being hit particularly hard. Sometimes, over 700 people might die in a single day. Other times, we are grateful when the reported numbers are "just" four or five hundred. Most days, I give the figures a quick glance and move on to the comics, the crossword puzzle, or the almost empty sports pages.

Until the Corona Virus took my uncle. Suddenly they weren't just numbers anymore.

Uncle Anthony was my mother's youngest brother and would have turned 75 this year. Although he didn't die alone, thanks to the true heroes working tirelessly to save his life 24 hours a day, he died without the benefit of his family to comfort him.

What can be worse, you ask, than losing a beloved family member to this devastating virus? Not being able to properly grieve with your family.

Our family has experienced its share of sorrow over my lifetime, just like any other family. My mother and father each had six brothers and sisters. That's a lot of aunts, uncles, and cousins. Growing up Italian, there is nothing more important than family. Backyard get-togethers are arranged, it seems, every time a new baby moves up a shoe size.

We even made jokes at first, when discussing why Italy was so hard hit by the virus. Way too much hugging and kissing going on over there, we laughed. Now, in our time of need, we can't grieve together.

There was plenty of crying and shock when we found out he

passed, but we couldn't reach out and hug anyone to try and console them. Instead of visiting with him at the hospital while providing love and support to my Aunt Joanne and cousins, we were forced to wait by the phone for daily updates. Unfortunately, so were they.

For our family, it's essential to gather and grieve when word spreads about a death in the family. We needed to be together. We needed to see each other. We needed to cry together, hug, and comfort each other as only family can.

Unfortunately, just like any other family trying to grieve during this crisis, you must grieve alone. The reports we were getting from the hospital varied each day. We were all optimistic that he might be able to pull out of it. You hope for the best but prepare for the worst.

A word to the wise; you are never prepared for the worst.

Now that he's gone, what are families supposed to do? There will be no viewing for family and friends at the funeral parlor. There will be no church ceremony that allows you to pray together. You can't even be together at the gravesite to say your final goodbyes. The Corona Virus just doesn't allow for it.

My wonderful Uncle Anthony, full of life, lost his fight sometime during the late afternoon of April 16th. That same day, 721 other New York families also lost loved ones. That's thousands of family members, just like ours, walking around like zombies, unsure of what to do next. Although they are forced to grieve alone, they are not alone.

Rest in Peace, my dear uncle. Although your earthly family couldn't be there when the Angel came to guide you, we are comforted in knowing that when you got there, your heavenly family would be awaiting your arrival.

MARRY AGAIN? DEPENDS ON WHO YOU ASK

2019

When you get together with your friends, many different things come up in the conversations.

My wife has often said that after taking care of the kids (and me) for most of her adult life, she would never get remarried if anything ever happened to me. Turns out she is not alone in that line of thinking.

Although most men indicated they would get married again, many long-time married women didn't share the same sentiment. We've been together for over 40 years, and I would miss her terribly if anything happened to her. I'm not sure what I would do without her.

Apparently, my wife (and many other women) all know precisely what they would do without us.

This column was submitted to the Press Club of Long Island for their 2020 Media Awards and helped me win Second Place in the "Narrative-Column" category.

Marry Again? Depends on Who You Ask
By Paul DiSclafani

A good friend of mine, after more than 20 years as a single mom raising two girls, has decided to take the plunge and give marriage a second chance. In all the years I've known her, she's never been happier. I have confidence that both she and her beau, who I've also known for a long time, will have many happy years ahead.

Just don't ask a woman who's been married for a long time if they would ever marry again; you might be surprised at the answer.

As a long-time married couple, we've had this conversation with our friends, many of whom have also been married for a long time. Maybe I'm being naive, but I was surprised that most, if not all the wives, agreed they would never get married again. Never, as in no possible way.

That doesn't mean they wouldn't welcome male companionship; they just wouldn't want them living with them. Rumor has it that senior men who can drive at night are considered quite an asset.

Don't get me wrong, I think they still love us; otherwise, we wouldn't have lasted this long. They just don't seem to want another one once we're gone. Statistically speaking, women outlive men, so they are willing to put up with us while we're still around. Maybe they are taking this "'til death do us part" thing way too seriously.

In a very informal survey of my male counterparts, most said just the opposite. They would absolutely marry again. Why is there such a disconnect between male and female views of married life after a spouse's death?

Most wives just don't want to take care of anyone anymore. All their lives, they've shouldered most of the load in child-rearing and, later in life, taking care of elderly parents. In between, there was us.

Men seem to want a special citation for clearing the dinner dishes or loading the dishwasher. If we complete a load of laundry all the way through folding and putting it away, we expect a parade in our honor. As for cleaning the bathroom, well, where is my Congressional Medal of Honor?

I get it. It may be 2019, but most long-term marriages are still following the blueprint from the '50s. Daddy works and fixes things around the house, and Mommy takes care of everything else. Except somewhere along the line, Mommy also went to work and took care of everything else while Daddy never really picked up the slack.

Only now, with the kids grown and Mommy and Daddy retired (or close to it), Mommy is still taking care of Daddy. It's no wonder they wouldn't sign up for that gig again.

For more than 60 years, I've always had someone to take care of me. Without my wife, I wouldn't be able to get out of the house in the morning. I'd turn into one of those guys who smells his clothes to see if he could wear them. I don't see any reason to ever make the bed again. There would be a lot of take-out and plastic utensils. I'd have multiple Roombas patrolling the floors to avoid vacuuming myself. And my bathroom? Sheesh.

My house would look like Ralph Kramden's apartment after Alice left him for calling her mother a "Blabbermouth." Even though Neil Young sang about a man needing a maid, I would need the companionship and the company.

Both my friends have been alone for a long time. After finding each other, I'm sure they'll work out the small details of household chores and take care of each other.

As far as our wives are concerned, they've already decided that life without us would not require a replacement husband. In a way, I know they've earned it. I just wish they weren't looking so forward to it.

Hey, honey, where are my reading glasses?

MY LITTLE LEAGUE NIGHTMARE STORY

2017

I like to bare my soul to my readers every now and then. I want them to get to know me, warts, and all. As a weekly columnist, I love telling stories about events in my life that I hope will make the reader laugh along with me.

This is one of those stories.

I have never been shy about my love for baseball even if, as an athlete, I was not that good at it. When my first son, James, was old enough for T-Ball, I couldn't wait for his first practice. I even offered my help to the manager as a coach.

At their first practice, the kids didn't even know which way to run down the base paths. Many of them had never even seen a baseball before. We put the kids out on the field to hit them some ground balls. It was comical, as you could imagine, with most of the kids still learning how to keep that giant glove from falling off their hand.

But when the manager shouted to the kids on the field, "Ok, let's get two!" I was shocked. These kids didn't even know where to stand, let alone what an "out" was. Yet this manager set them up to try and get a double play? What nonsense.

I vowed from that day forward to be the manager for both of my kids during their Little League days. I wanted them (and their teammates) to develop a love for the game and have fun along the way.

I've told this story to almost every team I coached.

My Little League Nightmare Story
By Paul DiSclafani

Spring is in the air, and in most hamlets on Long Island, it's time for Little League baseball.

I coached for more than a decade with the Massapequa International Little League while my children progressed through T-Ball, the Minors, the Majors, the Juniors, and even the Senior League. I enjoyed every minute of it, and to this day, most of the kids that came through my teams still call me "coach."

Some managers (and parents) felt that winning was important, but I always had a simple philosophy—everyone plays. My teams didn't win a ton of games (we won our share), but we had fun all the time. I showed them how to play the game the right way and that every player on the team was essential.

Of course, it always seemed to happen that one kid would be up with the bases loaded, only to strike out on three pitches. And why would the ball always find that kid in the outfield?

I spent a lot of time with the kids, talking about baseball, treating them like ballplayers. I preached that baseball was a team game and that every one of their teammates was special because we were all wearing the same uniform. We were a team.

Obviously, some kids were just better athletes than others. Some kids just weren't going to be the next Derek Jeter, no matter what you did for them.

I was one of those kids. I wasn't terrible, but I wasn't a star athlete. I couldn't judge a fly ball, but I was a solid infielder. I could hit, but my career average was probably close to the Mendoza Line (that's about .200 for you non-baseball fans).

I played in the era of parents not attending every game you played, or any game you played, for that matter. There were no water bottles, no team mother bringing juice boxes and orange slices. You just jumped on your bike, hooked your glove on your handlebars, and went to the game in your stinky, dirty uniform, wearing sneakers.

We didn't have our own bats, and we certainly didn't have our own helmets. We were lucky if, between both teams, we had four helmets, two of which were cracked. One was so big, Shaquille O'Neal could wear it. But we all had a love for the game.

One Saturday afternoon, my mother had invited most of my aunts and uncles for a barbeque, along with a large contingent of my cousins. Little Paulie (me) had an afternoon game, so everyone came to watch.

Sporting a freshly washed uniform, there I was, batting seventh and playing third base. In the second inning, I came up to bat and somehow fisted the ball into right field for a base hit. As I rounded first, everyone was cheering and yelling. I made my turn like a pro, returning to first base triumphantly. As I looked over to the bench area, everyone was waving and cheering for me.

We had advanced to the 90-foot bases the year before (I was now 14), so I tipped my cap to the adoring throng and cautiously took my lead off first base, staring down the pitcher with an intensity I had never shown before. I pondered stealing a base but had to concentrate and study his motion, making sure he didn't throw over and try to pick me off. Then the first baseman walked over to me, slapped his glove on my chest, and said, "You're out."

Oh no!

In horror, I looked over to the umpire, and he confirmed the indignity, saying only, "Yeah, you're out," holding up a fist with his thumb pointing upward. Apparently, the pitcher didn't have the ball at all. The first baseman did, and as soon as I left the base, he tagged me out.

There were about 100 or so feet between me and the bench; and unfortunately, there was no hole I could crawl into. It was the longest walk of shame in my young life.

I would tell that story to every one of my Little League kids that makes the last out of the game or misses the ball in the outfield to try and make them feel better. And it usually puts a smile on their face.

But almost 50 years later, I can still feel that tag.

MY MOTHER'S RETIREMENT PLAN

2019

My mother has always been a great source of material for my weekly column. A number of our conversations were turned into stories scattered throughout this collection.

For Mother's Day in 2019, I dedicated an entire column to her. For as long as I can remember, she has been carrying a yellowed newspaper clipping written by an anonymous author about his mother. It meant so much to her, I decided to give her something she could also cherish; only this was from me.

I thought about how mothers from her generation didn't generally have retirement plans since most never worked. I wanted her to know both my brother and I were her own retirement plan. She can withdraw from our services when she needs to without worry.

Towards the end of the column, I included the text from that anonymous author so she could get rid of that yellowed fragment of paper.

This is one of her favorite columns and is prominently displayed in a frame on the wall in her kitchen.

My Mother's Retirement Plan
By Paul DiSclafani

My mother received wonderful news recently regarding some health conditions that have been causing her more anguish than physical pain. She's very independent (sometimes too independent), still drives, and has a life of her own. She doesn't need my brother or me to take care of her on a day-to-day basis.

Our generation has been renamed the "Aging Baby Boomers" for a good reason. We're aging a lot faster than we want to, along with our parents. Many of us have already lost one, if not both parents. We lost our father a few years back; and quite frankly, I'm not ready to give up my mother. She still irons my work shirts.

Without a retirement plan to help her through the Golden Years, in my eyes, we are her retirement plan. Instead of depending on a monthly check, my mother can withdraw, without penalty, any service she requires.

She took care of us for all those years as kids and, as we got older, put in countless hours of babysitting, house cleaning, and meal production (she's Italian, you know). When it comes to taking care of her after a health issue or chauffeuring her to varying doctor appointments, we are invaluable to her. When she needs us, we will be there for her.

You know what keeps her up at night? Worrying that one of us might have to take a half-day off work to take her to an appointment. Whatever health problem she may have to endure, she worries more about disrupting our lives.

With Mother's Day right around the corner, give your mother the only gift she really wants, spending time with you. Don't just show up for dinner when invited; stop by when she's not expecting you. Call her every now and then for no reason at all, just to say hello. Think about what your lives will be like when your adult children are on their own and with their own families. How much are you going to miss them?

Let me offer an open letter to my mother from her boys:

Mom—You dedicated your life to us when we were young and taught us how to love and understand. You prepared us for this journey called life, picking us up when we were down and shining a light along the path when it was dark. You taught us how to appreciate music and laugh at The Honeymooners. Most importantly, you taught us how to respect ourselves and others. Without you or dad, we wouldn't be the men we are today.

So now it's our turn.

Helping when you need us is not disrupting anything. It's not an intrusion. You've earned that from us. This is one retirement plan that will never run out of capital.

There's a beautiful piece that is attributed to "unknown author" that I'd like to share:

Your Mother is always with you. She's the whisper of the leaves as you walk down the street. She's the smell of certain foods you remember, flowers you pick, the fragrance of life itself. She's the hand on the brow when you're not feeling well. She's your breath in the air on a cold winter's day. She is the sound of the rain that lulls you to sleep, she's the colors of the rainbow; she is Christmas morning. Your Mother lives inside your laughter. She's the place you came from, your first home, and she is the map you follow with every step you take. She's your first love, your first friend, even your first enemy, but nothing on earth can separate you. Not time, not space, not even death.

Mom, from the time we were babies, we looked up to you and dad. Now it is time for you to look up to us and know that you're in good hands.

Besides, who's going to iron my shirts?

THE HORROR OF LOSING YOUR CELL PHONE

2017

I'm a somewhat organized guy.

You might not realize it to look at my workspace. I like to refer to it as "organized chaos." You know the old phrase, "A place for everything and everything in its place?" I subscribe to that theory, but everything I own is usually wherever I look for it.

One of my all-time favorite television heroes was Oscar Madison. On many occasions, my mother has called me Oscar, considering I was a sportswriter, wore a Mets baseball hat, and loved to smoke cigars.

So, when I lost my cell phone, I was taken aback. The initial shock was quickly replaced by the horror of losing all my contacts and pictures.

Spoiler alert—I got the phone back, thanks to a Good Samaritan.

That touched off a series of arguments about whether the phone was actually lost or merely "misplaced."

The Horror of Losing Your Cell Phone
By Paul DiSclafani

I lost my cell phone.

Well, technically, I didn't know where it was, and someone found it; but in the end, I got it back. Does it count as a lost item if you get it back?

But the horror. The things that go through your mind before you finally connect that last dot and realize it's gone. You don't have it, and you don't know for sure where it might be.

You tap your pants pockets and check your jacket; where could it be? Quick—when was the last time you saw it? It's not on the floor or the seat of your car, so, where is it?

And while you are acting out your own *CSI* show in your head or wishing you had paid more attention to that old *Columbo* episode you saw on MeTV, the realization finally hits. You left it in the movie theater.

Oh, no, how could you be so stupid?

Now what? Are you even sure what theater you were in? Was it #5 or #7? Did you save your stub that has the theater number on it? There is most likely a completely different movie playing in that theater by now. How do you get back in there to check without looking like an idiot?

My goodness, when did this phone become such an essential part of our lives? People have risked death (and sometimes failed) trying to retrieve this device. And for what, the Contacts listing? Do you really need to recover all those selfies or pictures of your last dinner plate? Isn't that what "the cloud" is for? But "the cloud" can't help you now.

Actually, I've been on a Joe DiMaggio-type streak since I got my first phone, back when you had to pull out a little antenna to use it. I've never lost my phone, ever. I've had phones break or be damaged and needed to get a new one, but I've never lost it. I've misplaced it (who hasn't?) and had to search for it, but I never lost it and didn't get it back. My kids have lost their phones (skiing, at an amusement park), and my wife loses hers every three days (well, she usually finds it), but not me.

So I did what any self-respecting male would do in this situation: I panicked internally but was cool as a cucumber on the outside. I simply told my wife that I thought I might have left my phone in the movie theater. So, what's the first thing she says? "You lost your phone?"

Oh, the horror…

Although I disagreed with the term "lost," I didn't have too much of a leg to stand on at this point, so I just went with it as we tried to figure out what to do. She came up with the idea of using her phone to call mine to see if it would ring or buzz in the car somewhere. Maybe it was under the seat?

Just then, someone answered on the other end. A Good Samaritan had not only retrieved my phone but was doing everything in his power to reunite me with it. Even though the phone was locked, he could return a message to one of my friends (you just have to swipe it to the left, iPhone fans), who then contacted my brother. As she was hanging up with my new best friend, we got another call, this time from my brother. He wanted to tell us the same information we had just heard. Talk about synchronicity.

I met up with my hero at the Starbucks outside of the "Stadium 10" theatres in Farmingdale (he was sitting next to us during *King Kong - Skull Island*). He turned down my offer to buy him coffee as a reward. Still, I was humbled and forever grateful for his effort.

On the way home, I told my wife how close I had come to breaking my "never lost my phone" streak, but she disagreed with me. She said the phone was lost, and just because I found it doesn't negate the fact that it was lost, so the streak is over. I beg to differ. In my opinion, lost means lost; but once you find it, it's not lost anymore. I even looked it up in the dictionary: "unable to be found."

As far as I'm concerned, even though I had to suffer through the horror of misplacing my phone, I was able to recover it, so the streak continues.

Maybe I should look up exactly what "the cloud" does, you know, just in case.

MY STUPID HOUSE

2019

One afternoon at work, while sitting in a conference room waiting for a meeting to start, the conversation was drifting towards home technology. One of my coworkers told a story about how he was installing "smart" technology in his house.

He can now turn lights on and off using his smartphone from anywhere in the world. Another person chimed in about his new "Ring" doorbell, which notifies him on his phone if someone rings their doorbell.

When I was in Home Depot, I saw a refrigerator with a TV screen on the door that allowed you to look inside the fridge without opening the door. I even saw a Verizon FIOS commercial touting a remote control that you can speak into instead of pressing the buttons.

The absurdity of all the technological advancements led me to have a few laughs when I wrote this column.

"My Stupid House" took home Third Place in the 2020 Press Club of Long Island Media Awards for the category of "Humor Column."

. . .

My Stupid House
By Paul DiSclafani

Here's what we do in our house when we forget to leave a light on and walk in the front door. We reach over, flip up the light switch, and magically, the hallway light comes on. I don't have to open the door and politely ask my "smart house" to turn the light on.

I guess that makes my house stupid.

If my doorbell rings, I look through the glass in the door to see who's there. If it rings when I'm not home, no one is going to answer it except Louie the Labrador, who will bark loud and long enough for any thief to reconsider entering.

When I want more air conditioning, I hit the little arrow on the thermostat to lower the temperature and cool the house. The fact that my thermostat can also give me the weather forecast in Guam is irrelevant when I'm getting ready to go to sleep and want to be comfortable.

Of course, a smart house always needs an internet connection; and we all know how reliable that is. In my stupid house, I can still use my dishwasher by pressing the start button. I don't have to worry if I can't dim the dining room lights with my phone; I can just turn the knob to the left. I still have a CD player and a radio if I can't access my streaming music services.

Do I need to use my phone to check what's inside the refrigerator? If I find a cold beer, I still have to get up, open the door, grab the bottle, and open it. And I certainly don't need a video screen on the front so I can look inside. I can just open the door.

Let me tell you my idea of a smart house. When I'm in the shower, prevent anyone else from flushing the toilet or brushing their teeth, causing me to dance around scalding water. Want to impress me? Close the windows when it rains or change the color on the walls, so I don't ever have to paint again.

Is it really a technological advancement to speak into my remote control to change the channel? I guess having a device that can electronically send a signal from my couch to the TV when I press a button wasn't convenient enough for mankind. Forget about sanctioning the great minds of the 21st Century to cure diseases; let's make a remote control that doesn't need you to press buttons. What's next, blinking my eyes like "Jeannie" to change the volume?

Instead of being innovators, nobody seems to be making anything truly useful anymore. We've all become consumers and more interested in buying a new version of something that was already designed to make our lives easier. Why, in 2019, have we not made any real progress in offering affordable, aesthetically pleasing solar panels for homeowners who want to harness the power of the sun and reduce their dependence on electricity? Instead, we've created a couch that doubles as a Bluetooth speaker and a smokeless grill we can use indoors.

A person in their 80s today has lived through some of the greatest technological achievements mankind has ever seen, from the advent of electricity to space travel. What will children today see when we get close to the end of this century? The way we're going, there may not even be a need for them to get out of bed in the morning.

There were plenty of times I've gotten in bed and wished I'd shut the light off. I know if I really had a smart house, I could just pick up my phone and turn off the light without leaving my cozy bed.

Then again, for $19.95, all I would need to do is clap my hands twice, and my "clapper" will do it for me.

With or without an internet connection.

VACATIONING WITH AND WITHOUT THE KIDS

2017

These two columns were written while my wife and I vacationed at Universal Studios in Orlando Florida.

I submitted a few columns for the <u>Massapequa Observer</u> previously and was pleasantly surprised that they decided to publish them. Then I got an email from the editor asking me if I had a column for the next edition.

I was taken by surprise. First, I was in Florida with no access to a computer. Second, they were now asking me for content.

Could this be the start of me being published regularly, as a real columnist?

I knew that I couldn't tell them no. I might never get this opportunity again.

I excitedly read the email to my wife while we were having drinks at one of the Universal Studio City Walk bars. Now all I had to do was come up with a topic and, somehow, get it to the editor.

A couple our age was sitting at a table near us, smiling and enjoying their time together. I casually made eye contact with the gentleman who was also drinking a cocktail in an oversized souvenir glass. He lifted his glass toward me in a wordless salute to being on vacation.

I mentioned to my wife how great it was being on vacation without the kids. It got us talking about how sorry we felt for all those parents dragging *their kids from attraction to attraction. Here we were, sharing the same vacation spot with those families, but having a completely different experience.*

When we got back to the hotel, I went to the lobby and, using their public computer, banged out these two columns and submitted them to the editor. They were published in the next two editions.

The Massapequa Observer has published my column every week since then.

These two stories were published in the anthology A Trip for the Books (edited by JK Larkin) in 2020.

Vacationing With the Kids
By Paul DiSclafani

The lure of Disney World, or Orlando in general, is fairly enticing huddled in front of the TV while the temperature outside is brutal and snow is in the immediate future. Of course, watching those happy couples and their smiling children experiencing a personal meeting with a Disney Princess and having a front-row seat to the fireworks over the Magic Castle is everyone's dream vacation.

Only that's not what actually happens.

Taking young children to Disney World is a suicide mission. It will test your ability to remain civil to your children and each other. People just don't come to Massapequa anymore for its tourism since we closed the Massapequa Zoo more than 50 years ago, but they do head for the bright sunshine of Florida during the winter.

If you have spent time at JFK on departure day, you can see the happy faces of the families as they anticipate jetting to a wonderland of adventure. They already have their T-Shirts and funny hats on. Kids are reading books or playing with toys, just like angels. Kind of reminds me of the week leading up to Christmas—everyone is on their best behavior.

Then they arrive in Florida, and the adorableness level goes to 11. They are enjoying the weather, splashing around in the pool, and eating junk food. What could possibly go wrong? By this time tomorrow, you and your wife will be preparing your acceptance speeches for "Parents of the Year."

Don't rent that tuxedo just yet.

Now, I'm sure many of you have had wonderful experiences with your children at Disney World, Universal Studios, or Sea World while in Florida. I'll bet that you have wonderful pictures and memories that will last a lifetime. We've taken our children to Orlando several times as they grew from cherubic toddlers into moody teenagers. And I would say that about 60-70 percent of the time, it was a wonderful experience. But oh, the rest of the time was just brutal.

For all the planning and expense, nothing can prepare you for the actual experience of walking into a theme park while towing 100-pound backpacks and trying to control young children. Besides all the packing and preparation before you even leave the hotel room, once you get there, well, everyone else is there at the same time.

Do any of your children have any previous experience waiting in line for virtually anything? Do they have any conception of how long 30 minutes is when slowly shuffling along in the hot sun? Do they have any notion of how much things cost in a theme park? You will wind up saying the word "no" more times to your children in 10 hours than you will over the next 10 months.

But you know what? It costs you so much money to be at that theme park, you are determined to have a good time, even if you have to force them to have a good time. You will drag those children kicking and screaming from one attraction to another. And it doesn't matter what you want to do. It doesn't matter what your spouse wants to do. It doesn't even matter what your eldest children want to do. The only thing that matters is your youngest child, the lowest common denominator.

And when all is said and done, you lug your children, empty backpacks, and yourselves back to your hotel room, collapsing on the bed while they get a second wind and want to watch movies. It has been rough, but you made it.

Just think, only five more days to go.

Vacationing Without the Kids
By Paul DiSclafani

The last time we spoke, we talked about vacationing with our kids. Although I have always enjoyed the basic family vacation, it is always a lot harder on your wife in retrospect. They usually deal with the children all day long, and being on a vacation when you still take care of them doesn't seem fair, does it?

At a certain age, besides getting movie discounts, you've paid your dues and get to vacation without the kids. I know that sounds blasphemous to some of you, but trust me, it's not. Let's call it a perk, shall we?

You have endured countless hours dragging them from place to place, always returning to your 15'×20' hotel room more exhausted than you thought possible. Sometimes, it feels like you are stuck in the movie *Groundhog Day* for the next five days. There is hope, my friends.

A vacation without kids is even better than the awkwardness of your honeymoon. Now you actually know each other's likes and dislikes. You don't have to do anything to try to impress them or live up to some ridiculous "dream" honeymoon you saw on TV.

Feel like going to a theme park and experiencing all you missed because little Johnny was hot, tired, and hungry? Skipped reading all the interesting things on the wall when visiting NASA in Coco Beach because tiny Pamela was fussy? How about dragging half of the kids' worldly possessions across that pristine beach in the Bahamas, only to settle down and find out you forgot tiny Tim's inhaler on the dresser?

Yikes.

My wife and I have been on numerous vacations without our now adult children in the last few years, and I can honestly say, "My goodness—what took us so long?" Your main responsibility now is choosing what to have for breakfast and dinner.

Want to go to the pool? Grab your suit and go—no fuss, no muss. Will the rain in the forecast keep you indoors? As adults, you can, ahem, improvise. Want to have an adult beverage or two at the end of the day? Be my guest.

We just got back from a delightful week in Orlando, staying on the Portofino Bay property of Universal Studios. We went to the theme parks when (and if) we wanted, and then returned to the hotel every afternoon to spend the hot part of the day at the pool. After that, we thoroughly enjoyed dinner and drinks each evening, spending time in different places and enjoying the live music we found almost everywhere.

When vacationing without children, you tend to notice that all the other people vacationing without children are smiling most of the time. A simple nod or wink at strangers enjoying a drink at the bar, unencumbered with toddlers, confirms your kinship. Although we were free of our parental responsibilities, we did feel slight pangs of empathy for some of the other travelers.

Here we were, fresh as daisies, vibrant and alive, ready to boogie and enjoy the rest of our evening. There they were, those poor souls, dragging young children back to the hotel properties at the end of the day. Staring blankly with soulless eyes out into nothing, they sat motionless on the transportation systems. They were hoping beyond hope that little Bobby would cooperate and be quiet until they could get back to the hotel and change that diaper. All the time, knowing they would have to do it all over again the next day.

Waiter, I'll have another Blue Hawaiian, and my wife will have another Hurricane.

I'M UNPREPARED FOR THE APOCALYPSE

2017

A man must know his limitations, and I certainly know mine.

I know I'm not going to be a survivor when the apocalypse finally hits. I don't like to go camping. I need my creature comforts. Just the thought of going a few hours without electricity gives me the willies.

With that said, we were out in Montauk with some friends and family. While sitting around the fire one evening, I was fascinated by my cousin Denise's husband Hugo and his fire-making skills. He took complete control of creating the fire pit in the sand, placing the logs precisely right, and getting the fire started in no time.

Some people are made to live outdoors; and when the time comes and we are forced to live like cavemen again, Hugo will be King.

This humorous column helped Long Island Living *win its first award from the Press Club of Long Island in their 2018 Media Awards contest, as my column placed Third in the "Narrative-Column" category. This essay was also part of the Red Penguin Collection* It's The End of the World as We Know It, *published in 2021 and edited by JK Larkin.*

I'm Unprepared for the Apocalypse
By Paul DiSclafani

Many people in this country are terrified of some sort of apocalyptic event occurring, giving birth to a reality show on the National Geographic Channel called *Doomsday Preppers*. People are already preparing for the apocalypse.

None of them are zeroing in on a specific apocalyptic event, like zombies or an alien invasion. Still, everything seems to revolve around the complete and total breakdown of society. The loss of electricity and public utilities will inevitably lead to anarchy. The preppers are ready to defend their possessions and amass enough supplies to survive in a world without order or a Wal-Mart.

Here on Long Island, we tend to lean a little too heavily on our public utilities to survive. Many of us bought generators after Superstorm Sandy in 2012 because we never want to be without electricity again—even for 24 hours. We waited hours in line for gas because we couldn't live without our cars or didn't want to miss an episode of *The Office*.

Long Island is home to many campgrounds where you can choose to live the life of our pioneering settlers, sans electricity and some amenities. You make campfires and cook in cast iron pans. Of course, you also spend a week preparing for your journey back in time, making sure you have marshmallows and chocolate bars for s'mores. Don't forget your coffee and milk.

But what if you suddenly had to live the life of our ancestors tomorrow? Are you prepared to "go camping" for six months or a year?

I know I'm not.

While out in Montauk, I was with my cousin's husband Hugo, who is prepared for anything. He can make fire and carries a knife that does hundreds of things. He can catch, clean, and cook anything that walks or swims. Hugo will survive for years after the apocalypse hits.

I need air conditioning and a TV.

I need a bed and a toilet.

I need a roof.

I know I'm not going to survive the apocalypse. As a matter of fact, I'm not even going to try. Zombies eating humans? No problem, where's the BBQ sauce? Do you want me rare or well done?

I watch *The Walking Dead*. I won't survive out in the open eating berries and drinking rainwater. When the food supply from 7-11 runs out, I'm history. Besides, they walk everywhere on that show. Did the zombies eat all the bicycles, too?

Okay, so a zombie apocalypse is ridiculous. What happens if the national grid goes off-line again, but this time for a year or more? You think you can survive as our ancestors did in the 1800s? Even if you knew how to do it, there's not enough livestock on Long Island to slaughter. There will be no more ice cubes.

Do you know what the average life expectancy in the United States was in 1850? It was 39. You know why? People lived off the land, and there were no walk-in doctor clinics if you got the sniffles. You got sick, you died.

Trust me, that hooey about the meek inheriting the earth is nonsense. No, my friends, only the strong will survive; but the lunatics will thrive. I don't want any part of that.

When the apocalypse hits, 95 percent of the population, like me, will be ill-prepared for it. Not only are we unprepared, but we're also not going to survive. Think about how upset you get when the cable goes out on Friday, and the repairman isn't scheduled to get to you until Tuesday. You think you're surviving while walking around in the same outfit for three weeks as you try to catch a wild squirrel with the cord from your iPhone? Most of us can't survive three hours in the dark without power, needing flashlights to get from the kitchen to the bedroom.

Not me, count me out. I admit it. I might be the most ill-prepared person on Long Island to survive on my own.

Unless, of course, I can get a taxi to take me to Hugo's house.

MY UNCLE SAMMY THE WAR HERO

2017

This story took me on a journey I never expected to take.

I had heard bits and pieces of this story from relatives on my father's side for most of my life. Salvatore DiSclafani (Sammy) was my father's older brother and the firstborn in the family.

My dad was just 14 years old (he was the youngest of seven) when Sammy was killed in Italy during World War II. As the family told the story, he and his platoon were captured behind enemy lines in occupied Italy and killed by German soldiers. The horrific details of the story were unknown at the time, other than they were forced to dig their own graves before being killed.

The soldier's execution was ordered by German General Anton Dostler. He was captured by the Americans and the first of many Germans to be convicted of War Crimes. He was sentenced to death in 1945. Many of my relatives still have the front page of the Daily News, showing Dostler with his hands tied behind his back and a black hood over his head, slumping forward from the wooden pole he was anchored to.

A few years before I started writing this column, I met up with a friend at work who was a World War II buff. I asked him if he knew anything about Anton Dostler and told him the story, limited as it was, about my Uncle

Sammy. One thing led to another, and he soon found some details about my uncle's mission.

I questioned every one of my aunts and uncles. Still, nobody seemed to know anything more, not even the reason for the mission or how he became a part of it. With the power of the Internet at my fingertips, I began doing my own research.

I learned my Uncle Sammy was a part of the OSS, the Office of Strategic Services, and a precursor to the CIA. I found that he was on a secret mission to go behind enemy lines in occupied Italy and blow up a railroad tunnel off the Ligurian Coast, near Framura. I found a book by Joseph Squatrito, <u>Code Name: Ginny</u>, chronicling the entire mission. Squatrito's uncle Rosario was one of the 15 soldiers in my uncle's platoon.

Between all of the reference material I uncovered, I was able to piece together most of the story. Talking to some of my relatives about it (my father had already passed), jogged some deep-seated memories and confirmations. They found documents and letters from the government to confirm the story.

I had been writing my column for about five months when Memorial Day came around in 2017. Instead of writing a column, I wanted to tell my readers a story. I wanted them to understand what a true hero looks like. I wanted them to see what a sacrifice these young men made to rid the world of terror.

It is unlike any column I have ever written and one that I am most proud of.

Somehow, this article made its way overseas and was used by an Italian writer who reached out to me while researching the Ginny missions and the aftermath. She and I have become email pals over the years. She even invited me to attend a 2019 ceremony in Italy commemorating the 75th Anniversary of the mission. Although I couldn't attend, she asked me to send a short piece, which she read at the ceremony.

In 2019, someone from the Italian American Studies Association (Long Island Chapter) read the article and asked me to attend one of their monthly meetings and meet the members. They invited me to be their guest speaker at their Annual Dinner in June of 2020 to read the column and have a Q&A with the audience. Unfortunately, COVID canceled that dinner.

I have requested that my editor run this story every year around Memorial Day, as a tribute to those heroes.

Who knows? This story might make a great novel someday...

My Uncle Sammy, the War Hero
By Paul DiSclafani

The early morning darkness of March 22, 1944, was cloudy with no moonlight to guide the three inflatable boats carrying 15 United States soldiers. They were on a secret mission almost 250 miles behind enemy lines on the rocky Ligurian coast near Framura, in occupied Italy. The soldiers paddled towards the shore with 650 pounds of dynamite in tow. Their mission: to locate and destroy two train tunnels, where the Genova-La Spezia lines joined together to meet the seashore. These rail lines were the main supply arteries to Anzio.

These well-trained soldiers had volunteered for duty in the newly formed Office of Strategic Services (OSS). They were chosen for this specific mission because of their Italian heritage and their ability to speak Italian to some degree. My father's oldest brother, my uncle Sammy DiSclafani (whose given name was Salvatore), was one of those soldiers. They had previously tried this same mission, code name "Ginny," on a similar moonless night in February but could not locate the target. Additional aerial surveys enabled them to make a second attempt in a new mission, dubbed "Ginny II."

Without the benefit of PT boat radar and unable to communicate with the ships due to unreliable radio transmissions that night, ocean currents caused the commandos to drift off-course. To make matters worse, the PT boats were forced to vacate their position and abandon the commandos when German torpedo boats appeared.

On land but unable to locate their target as dawn approached, they hunkered down in an unoccupied farmhouse to hide for 24 hours, as per the mission directive. On the morning of the 23rd, two officers left on a reconnaissance mission for food and information, successfully locating the Genova-La Spezia target. Now all they had to do was coordinate their escape with the PT boats after they blew the tunnel and completed their mission later that evening.

But both PT boats ran into trouble, one with a mechanical breakdown and the other encountering enemy activity, and were forced to turn back. Without a viable escape plan, the mission would have to wait another day.

Little did they know they had just 72 hours to live.

Unfortunately, the uniformed soldiers were spotted by an Italian girl who notified authorities. They were captured and surrendered that morning, March 24. After being initially interrogated by Fascist Italian authorities, they were turned over to the German military and transferred to the 135th Fortress Brigade in La Spezia.

Now in the Germans' hands, the interrogations went to another level, revealing their mission's true nature. Once identified as a commando raid, the situation was relayed up the German hierarchy. The next morning, March 25, a cable arrived signed by General Anton Dostler. The Americans were to be executed immediately, as per an edict implemented by Adolph Hitler in 1942. The Fuhrer Befehl Commando Order specified immediate death without trial for anyone engaging in sabotage behind German lines. Although the German officers knew that executing uniformed prisoners of war was a direct violation of the Geneva Convention, they had sworn a loyalty oath to Hitler.

On the morning of March 26, the 15 Italian-American soldiers, still in uniform, were brought to a remote location, Punta Bianca, on the Ameglia peninsula's hilltop. They were executed and then buried in a shallow, hidden grave, as the German military sought to cover up their war crimes. A German communique was issued that the commandos had been killed in combat; and just a few days later, all written records of the incident were destroyed.

There is no happy ending to this story unless you count General Dostler being captured and tried before an American Military Commission in October of 1945. He was the first German general brought to trial after the war. His defense of "obeying orders" was rejected, which contributed to Principle IV's creation for future Nuremberg war crime trials. The legal defense of "supervisor orders" was deemed unacceptable. Dostler was found guilty and executed by firing squad on December 1, 1945.

As we celebrate Memorial Day with barbeques and car sales, I share this story to remind us what sacrifices the men and women in our military make every day.

Some people call Derek Jeter or Tom Brady heroes. I wanted you to know the story of my Uncle Sammy and the other 14 men who volunteered for this mission, not knowing if they were ever going to see their families again. They all posthumously received the "Silver Star," but they didn't do it for the glory; they did it for their country and what they believed in.

They did it for all of us. That's the true definition of a hero.

MAKE MINE A WHOPPER

2019

There are times when you read an article or have a conversation about something that ends up going in a completely different direction than you expected. This column was one of those times.

As a kid, fast food was not only your meal of choice; it was your only choice. Of all the fast-food restaurants, I was always a Burger King fan. Since you could always "have it your way," we would take advantage and ask for extra "everything."

Having stupid conversations with your friends was also a way of life back then. Every now and then, the subject of "what would you order for your last meal if you were on death row" would come up.

Although I don't remember the details of those conversations, I was always fascinated with the subject. As an adult, pondering the menu for the last meal of your life was a heavy subject and not for the faint of heart. Oh, sure, you could make light of the issue and give a careless answer. But if you really put yourself in the shoes of a guy on death row, what would you choose?

When I read about a recent Texas execution, they mentioned inmates were no longer allowed to choose their last meal. That seemed unfair, but it was wholly justified after I did some research. That research led me to the "last meal" rules in some other states. Before I knew it, I had the workings of an interesting column.

Still, I have often thought about those last meal choices and what I might choose...

Make Mine a Whopper
By Paul DiSclafani

The state of Texas executed a convicted murderer who spent more than 20 years behind bars. He was the fourth death row inmate killed in the United States this year, with another 17 waiting their turn.

Wait, don't leave yet. This column isn't meant to stimulate a political discussion about the pros and cons of capital punishment. It's intended to encourage an entirely different discussion.

What would you request for your last meal?

During interviews, most celebrities contemplate massive feasts with lobster, caviar, and champagne (although alcohol is not allowed). That's not what most prisoners request. Instead, they seek comfort food like steak or fried chicken.

Can a prisoner request anything? Sure, but that doesn't mean they're going to get it. In Florida, for example, the meal can't cost more than $40 and must be prepared locally. Sorry, no croissants from France. Some states only offer what can be cooked in the prison's kitchen.

On the other hand, Texas no longer allows death row inmates the option of making a request. They get whatever was on that day's menu. Most Texas inmates prefer not to be executed on a Tuesday; they hate meatloaf night.

Back in 2011, a Texas death row inmate named Larry Brewer submitted the most elaborate last meal request ever: a triple-meat bacon cheeseburger, three fajitas, a pound of BBQ, a half-loaf of white bread, Meat Lover's pizza, a pint of Blue Bell vanilla ice cream, a slab of peanut butter fudge with crushed peanuts, and three root beers. Larry's request was granted, and as a final protest, he didn't eat any of it. That didn't sit well with elected officials, who stopped the practice entirely.

Thanks, Larry; you've ruined it for everybody!

Serial killer John Wayne Gacy got fried shrimp and a bucket of KFC with French fries, while Timothy McVeigh, The Oklahoma City Bomber, skipped dinner entirely and had two pints of ice cream. Ted Bundy declined to request a last meal, so the serial killer got the standard last meal by default: steak, eggs, hash browns, toast, milk, and juice. Sounds more like breakfast at IHOP.

Many moons ago, my friends and I pondered that question. After a night of, well, let's call it, "adult activities," we usually ended the evening at a diner or a fast food joint that was still open. We spent way too much time having ridiculous discussions at places like Burger King, McDonald's, White Castle, Taco Bell, and Jack-in-the-Box.

So, what would you request? Choose wisely, my friend. If it's my last meal, I'm taking no chances with someone else picking out my steak and possibly overcooking it. What am I going to do, send it back? Unless my mother could make me a plate of spaghetti and meatballs, I'm not trusting anybody else's sauce. Most Italians won't order pasta in a restaurant for a reason. Never was a big fish fan; what if I choke on a fishbone?

I'd have a simple request. I want to go out with a Burger King Whopper and fries, washing it down with a tall glass (or two) of coke with ice. I want an order of diner-style onion rings, the real rings dipped in batter. I want A1 Sauce to mix into ketchup for dipping the onion rings. I'd also like a breast and wing from KFC, extra crispy. No vegetables, thank you. I spent my life eating vegetables only because I had to.

When I'm all done with dinner, I want a big piece of NY-style cheesecake and some mint chocolate chip ice cream on the side. A cup of Dunkin' Donuts coffee with cream (no sugar) would be nice.

I know it's macabre to think about something like your last meal, but I want to be prepared, just in case.

Wait, don't I get a snack? What about a Snickers before I take that long walk?

THE DEATH OF THE CAPED CRUSADER

2017

It's no secret that as we age, our childhood idols age along with us, although most of them had a pretty good head start. Although their performances are preserved forever in our memory (and, apparently, on Netflix, Hulu, YouTube, and other platforms), it is still a shock when they pass.

When Adam West, TV's Batman, passed in 2017, a part of my childhood died with him. Others portrayed Batman in the movies, but West was my Batman. Just like George Reeves was my Superman.

Guess we'll have to file this under, "Nothing lasts forever."

Goodbye, old chum…

The Death of the Caped Crusader
By Paul DiSclafani

If you were a nine-year-old growing up in 1966, the TV series *Batman* was your life, and Adam West was your Batman. West recently passed away at the age of 88.

In the age when most Long Island families had just one black and white television, there weren't a lot of options for kids after dinner.

There were only a handful of channels to select from (2, 4, 5, 7, 9, and 11) and evening television was geared toward adults.

TV for kids was mostly limited to weekend cartoons and afternoon reruns, but Wednesday night at 8:00 p.m.? You watched whatever your parents were watching.

Then came *Batman*, unlike any other TV program at the time. It was made for kids but with a wink and a nod to the adults in the room. We didn't understand the nuances of all the dialogue or cheesy puns. We weren't familiar with the "guest stars" appearing as villains or concerned citizens, sticking their heads out of windows as Batman and Robin scaled apartment buildings. It was described as "campy" at the time, but what does a nine-year-old know of campy?

Batman and his sidekick, the Boy Wonder, were crime fighters. There was a cool Bat-cave with computers and epic battles against the main villain's henchmen with cool "Whap," "Biff," and "Oooooff" graphics to accentuate the punches. *Batman* even had a cool theme song, with pounding drums and an infectious melody that sticks with you even today. And that car. There isn't a man over 50 that wouldn't give his right arm to just sit in that black Batmobile with the red stripes just once.

What made *Batman* unique was the adventure unfolded over two consecutive nights. Wednesday's episode ended in a cliffhanger, with Batman and Robin in an impossibly ridiculous trap, about to be blown up, burned alive, or vaporized. How were they going to get out of this one?

Holy cliffhanger, Batman!

Sitting frozen on the floor while staring at the tube, the narrator would tease us about the perilous situation at hand. Finally, he'd utter the words that would become part of the television lexicon, "Tune in tomorrow. Same Bat-Time, same Bat-Channel."

Tomorrow? We'd have to wait for tomorrow while our heroes were chained upside down, slowly being lowered into a vat of acid?

There was no better parental motivator on Thursday afternoon than, "If you don't get your homework done, you're not watching

Batman tonight." It was way more effective than, "Wait until your father gets home." You bet that math homework got done.

Batman wasn't a "superhero" with some sort of mutant power. He was just a mortal guy, albeit a rich mortal guy, who built cool weapons to help him fight crime. He drove a cool car with a secret identity and a sidekick and had a secret crime-fighting lab hidden inside a cave.

Batman lasted just three television years, 1966 to 1968, but made 120 episodes. In today's world, 120 episodes would spread out over 10 seasons and probably 15 years in duration.

The *Batman* TV series remained popular with kids because it never outgrew the target audience. It was three years, twice a week, and their pre-teen audience was still in their pre-teens when it was canceled. Apparently, the 8-11 demographic was not desirable enough for advertisers. What other crime fighter could defeat villains with his intellect while taking the time to correct his partner's grammar and make sure he uses his seatbelt?

Today's generation knows Batman as "The Dark Knight" and Adam West as the Mayor of Quahog on *Family Guy*. To my generation, West will always be "The Caped Crusader," a crime-fighting hero with a tiny utility belt that holstered numerous gadgets and gizmos to get them out of trouble. West's Batman was a hero kids could look up to and emulate without mutant powers.

When I heard the news of Adam West's passing, all I could think of was, "Holy Heartbreak." As West joins Alfred the butler, Bat Girl, and Commissioner Gordon in the great beyond, there are also villains from the TV show waiting for him, like the Riddler, the Joker, and the Penguin.

What's going to happen next? Guess we'll have to wait for tomorrow, same Bat-time, same Bat-channel.

LOUIE THE LABRADOR SPEAKS OUT

2020

In the early days of the COVID-19 Pandemic, there were many unanswered questions about what you could and could not do. People, including your humble narrator, were frightened.

Many people worked from home and were self-isolating. They escaped by walking their dogs. I immediately turned my attention to our Labrador, Louie.

My wife takes Louie on long walks every day, so his life was no different during the Pandemic. The most significant disruption to his life was me being home every day. I started to think about what might be going through his doggie brain and thought it would be fun to share his thoughts with my readers.

This column helped "Long Island Living" win First Place for the category "Narrative-Column" in the 2021 Press Club of Long Island Media Awards.

Louie the Labrador Speaks Out
By Paul DiSclafani

In these days of social distancing, we can't be too confident about what we can and cannot do. So, to be sure, I'd like to keep you safe from any possible contamination while you enjoy this column. I've asked a household member that's immune from contracting the Coronavirus (as far as we know) to step in and help.

I asked Louie the Labrador to take over this week, and here's what has been on his mind the last few weeks.

I'm not quite sure I understand what's going on, but things have certainly been a little strange around here lately. Usually, my girl and I go for a nice morning walk. Then, I have the run of the house while she goes to see that stupid horse. Sorry Stormy, I know I shouldn't be jealous, but I hate to share her with anybody. I go anywhere I want, and my only worry is when that vacuum machine turns on every afternoon and travels all around the house. It seems like every time I move to a different room, it follows me. Man, I hate that thing.

But lately, when we get home, I find that guy in my favorite room. I can still sit on the chair and look outside to make sure things are going smoothly; but this is supposed to be my quiet, alone time.

Now, I have to put up with loud music in my room as he sits in front of that little box with the light coming from it, tapping on it all day long. I'm not sure, but I keep hearing the same music over and over. I listened to the girl once tell him he's stuck in 1978, whatever that means.

Although he never takes me on a walk, he does like to sit with me out on the porch for a few hours every now and then. Except, he's always got some fire stick in his mouth, and it smells like, well, you know. I hate those things, but there's no escape for me. I'm collared and leashed, you know.

I heard from my friend Otto Von BisBark. He's a tiny Schnauzer the size of my chew toy. His people are starting to get bored and are dressing him in outfits while putting sunglasses on his head. Don't people know we're not playthings? I hope my people don't start doing that to me. Otto said his mug would be plastered all over something called 'Instagram' and 'Facebook.' Don't people understand we hate getting dressed up in costumes? Haven't they noticed that every time you see a picture of a dog dressed as Batman, the dog's tail is never wagging in happiness?

To be honest, it's not all that bad. In fact, I'm getting a lot more attention. Lots of belly rubs, plenty of treats, and everyone is at my beck and call. In, out, in, out, in, out. I'm loving this. And the foot traffic out in the streets has certainly picked up. My girl walks me every day, but now there are so many other dogs out with their people. There are new smells everywhere.

If anything, I'm glad they don't leave me at night anymore. They used to go out by themselves every now and then, but that seems to have stopped. If there's anything I hate, it's when they say, 'Be a good boy and watch the house.' What do they think I do all day long? Also, I don't know why other people haven't been coming over anymore. I get so excited when people visit because that means extra pats on my head, belly rubs, and, most importantly, food thingy's falling on the floor all the time. I miss that most of all."

Thanks for filling in, Louie. Please accept my apology. I had no idea you hated cigars.

Stay safe, dear readers.

REMEMBERING MY FATHER

2018

My father passed away in 2010. He was my biggest fan and would have loved to read these columns every week. I had never written a column specifically about him before.

It took a black-and-white photograph I posted on Facebook in 2018 to make me realize how much I missed him.

I believe this picture was from a place called "Frontier Town" in upstate New York, a Western-themed attraction. We could drive there for the afternoon and come back the same day.

This is one of the most emotional columns I have ever written. I re-post it on Facebook every Father's Day as a tribute to my dad, along with the picture.

Now, when I see this picture, it brings back all the emotion of this column. Sorry, I need a Kleenex...

Remembering My Father
By Paul DiSclafani

Another Father's Day has come and gone. After a morning of being pampered at Happy Feet, I spent the evening with my family, barbecuing steaks and chicken. In between, I relaxed in my backyard with a Coors Light and a nice cigar my friend George gave me.

As most people my age do in 2018, I perused my Facebook newsfeed to see what others were up to. Facebook was flooded with pictures and tributes to dads, mostly those that have passed. Not to be outdone, I dusted off a black and white photograph my mother took of my dad and me when I was about three and a half.

In a moment frozen in time, we were sitting on a bench at some western-themed attraction. I held a hot dog in my hand, and there was a wooden fence behind us surrounding a horse barn. My father is sporting a tiny cowboy hat on his head that I must have been wearing at some point during the day. It's one of my favorite pictures of all time.

When posting it on my timeline, I added the text, "To all the dads out there, for taking the time to wear the little hat."

That's when I realized I was crying.

My father has been gone for almost 10 years now, and I've done my share of privately weeping about it over the years. I don't think I loved or missed my father any more than anyone else who has lost theirs over time, so I'm not looking for any sympathy. Although I still weep when I see Cleon Jones catch the last out of the 1969 World Series or Bob Nystrom score that Stanley Cup-winning goal in 1980, I'm not sure where this wave of emotion came from or why. I've seen this photo hundreds of times.

My dad always took an interest in what my brother and I were doing. He was especially proud if we were ever recognized for anything we did in life. He would keep tiny newspaper clips if our names appeared, even for the most trivial things, like a Little League story blurb. I once wrote a freelance story about dog sled racing on Long Island that *Newsday* published in 1980 (the only non-school article that I had ever gotten published). He treasured that article and would show it to people like I had won a Pulitzer Prize. Sometimes I would get a letter to the editor published in *Newsday* or *The Daily News*, which would go into his private stash.

I know how much he would have loved reading this column every week. I also know that he would have been one of my greatest sources of material. There is a little bit of him (and my mother) in almost every column I write.

When I found out I had been nominated for a 2018 Press Club of Long Island Award as a columnist a few weeks ago, I thought about how he would have reacted to the news. Everyone in his world would have gotten a phone call. Even though it was a great honor for me to take home third place against journalists from all over Long Island (including *Newsday*), I know he would have been so proud. His eyes would have filled with tears every time he told someone about it.

Like father, like son, right?

It got me thinking about how he was always there for us, no matter the situation. My father could always make things right. That day the picture was taken, my mother said I was being a real pill and didn't want to wear the cowboy hat anymore. So being a good dad, he stepped up to the plate and wore the little hat for me. Not every father would do that, but mine did.

This one's for you, dad.

GOOD GRIEF, A SURPRISE ARRIVES IN THE MAIL

2017

I don't get a lot of tickets for traffic violations. My wife was a New York City Police Officer for 22 years, so, on occasion, I've pulled out my "Get out of Jail Free" card to avoid a ticket or two.

I remember the first time I ever had to use it. My wife was on the job for only a few weeks when I slid through a stop sign in Massapequa and was flagged down by a Nassau County Police Officer. I calmly showed the officer my license, conveniently located right next to the courtesy card in my wallet billfold.

He took both the license and the courtesy card and, after taking a deep breath, waived the card in my face and admonished me, "This is not a license to break the law."

When I told my wife about it, I got an earful from her, as well. Needless to say, I've been on my best behavior ever since, although the card has saved me a few times over the last 35 years.

But not this time. The anonymity of the Red-Light Camera summons has changed all that. The new robotic arm of the law knows nothing of courtesy, only of violation. You break the law, you get a ticket. End of story.

This column was part of the package I put together for the 2018 Press Club of Long Island Media Awards. It helped <u>Long Island Living</u> take Third Place in the "Narrative-Column" category.

Good Grief, A Surprise Arrives in the Mail
By Paul DiSclafani

Things were going so well.

The summer had been cruising along. I'd seen a few good movies, even a concert or two. Naturally, as July turns to August, we all lament how brief the summer is and vow to make the most of the final month.

Sitting on the porch with Louie the Labrador, enjoying the tranquility with a fresh Cup of Joe, we were listening to Steely Dan Radio on Pandora when the mood was broken by the approaching mailman. Louie and the mailman don't seem to get along, but then again, it's Louie's job to protect the house and announce, with authority, that someone is approaching.

Amongst the usual bills and unwanted solicitations was a letter I almost dismissed as junk mail—Red Light Safety Program. It was a red-light camera violation, and it was addressed to me.

Oh no.

Staring at the envelope, I knew it had to be a mistake. Inside was a document containing several photos of my car in various time lapses. The car seemed to be making a right turn on red at the corner of Conklin and Route 110 in Farmingdale. The citation was a month old, and, quite frankly, I can't even remember being in that area. I checked the calendar and found out it was a Sunday afternoon.

What would I be doing at that corner on a Sunday?

It was certainly my car, it was certainly making a right on red, and I assume it was me behind the wheel. The photos clearly showed my brake lights on. Now, I'm angry. I don't mind getting a ticket if I violate the law and get stopped by a police officer—they are doing their job. But this? This is an intrusion of my privacy. Maybe they purposely take a month to notify you, so you have no recollection and therefore can't dispute it. How can you dispute what you don't even remember doing?

Dispute it anyway you say? Of the 411,008 citations issued in

Suffolk County in 2015, barely 2 percent of drivers disputed them and only 0.09 percent had them dismissed. You have a better chance of being struck by lightning.

Not only is there a $50 fine, but they also tack on a $30 "administration fee." What is that all about? According to the citation, "A $30 administration fee will be added to all violations occurring on or after April 1, 2013." What catastrophic event occurred before April 1, 2013, requiring an additional $30 administration fee on every red-light violation since? What are we doing here, buying concert tickets through Ticketmaster?

Wait a minute—there's a link in the notice to the actual video of the violation. This is going to prove once and for all that I made a stop before making that right. Maybe I will be able to dispute it after all, even with a 0.09 percent success rate. As Han Solo once said, "Never tell me the odds."

Watching the video jogged my memory. Of course! I was heading to the seafood place across from Republic Airport to get lobster tails for a barbecue. I can see my car approaching the corner, the light was already red, but I was making the turn, so I slowed down and, and, and…

Guilty as charged.

Man, this started out to be such a nice morning; now I'm getting depressed. Guess Big Brother is truly watching. Finally accepting my fate, I clicked on the link to pay the fine. Of course, there is an additional $4 fee to pay online.

In just an hour, I went through all five stages of grief: denial, anger, bargaining, depression and, finally, acceptance. After putting $84 on my credit card, I went back out to the porch to sit with Louie. While all this craziness had been going on, he still seemed to be relaxing and enjoying Steely Dan on a beautiful Saturday morning. He might as well have been sleeping on the top of a doghouse.

Good grief, Charlie Brown.

TIME TO RETHINK HOW WE CELEBRATE WEDDINGS?

2020

I hit a nerve with this column.

The COVID Pandemic forced the cancellation of numerous wedding ceremonies at banquet halls, golf courses, and castles. Many couples had their dreams of a big wedding ruined, or at least postponed.

So, I posed the question - Do young couples, just starting out, really need all the aggravation and cost associated with a vast, over-the-top wedding? Maybe it's time to cut back on these extravaganzas? After all, a wedding reception is supposed to gather friends and family to help the bride and groom begin their lives together.

After attending (and participating in) five or six of our friends' weddings, my wife and I decided to buck tradition and make ours different. My wife didn't want to saddle her bridesmaids with unwearable gowns, so she chose different colors and a light, breezy (and inexpensive) style out of the JC Penney Catalog. Instead of a lavish ballroom, we chose a private room at a VFW Hall. We decided on a buffet-style dinner instead of a sit-down dinner. After all, the cocktail hour at every wedding is always better than a meal. Why not just have a giant cocktail hour where people can eat what they want? Instead of the expense of a band playing the music we love, we had a DJ spin the actual records.

Instead of a wedding, we decided to have a party.

Back in 1983, this was unheard of. But to this day, people tell me this was the most fun they ever had at a wedding.

Some young couples in our family planned wedding receptions in 2020 but decided on the ceremony only. Their "reception" would take place in 2021 on their first anniversary. Others just decided to do something simple and call it a day.

Either way, the happy couples are married and well on their way to a happy life together. And isn't that what it is all about, anyway?

Time to Rethink How We Celebrate Weddings?
By Paul DiSclafani

Raise your hand if some of the weddings you attended recently were a little over the top.

In recent years, we've attended weddings held in Castles and giant ballrooms. They were so outrageously extreme, we thought about adding a few hundred dollars to the gift envelope. The amount of food available in the cocktail hour alone was enough to feed a small town.

The entertainment sometimes included not just a DJ spinning bass-thumping music but video screens. At one reception, the video crew was able to show us a slickly produced music video of the actual wedding ceremony that happened earlier in the day. It even included showing the bride and groom entering the reception hall just an hour or so before. We got to see ourselves on video while the reception was still going on.

Don't get me wrong. If this is your idea of a dream wedding, and you have a seemingly unlimited cash flow, do what you want; however, you want. Use those classic limos from decades ago or horse-drawn carriages. It's your party and, as far as I am concerned, there is no line you can't cross.

At a wedding a few years back, there was a dessert hour that followed a huge dinner. Fourteen separate dessert stations came rolling out of the kitchen like endless clowns emerging from a Volkswagen, each containing different delicious treats. There were cookies, cakes, ice cream sundaes, and cotton candy. They formed a rectangle around the dance floor, each station with its own server. Once all the carnage was complete, and everyone had their fill, the wedding cake and coffee came out.

As my Italian relatives might say, "Oooh-Fa!"

If this pandemic has taught us anything, it has shown us we can do without a lot of things. We've learned to live without live sporting events and going to movie theaters. Suddenly, eating restaurant quality take out at home is not a bad option anymore. Going to a gym to run on a treadmill is an expensive novelty we can do without.

Many planned 2020 weddings were ultimately postponed. Those couples might have learned they don't need a giant banquet room with hundreds of people to celebrate with them on their wedding day. They just need each other and their close families.

When you think about it, that's not a bad option.

No matter the size of your wedding, when the dust settles and everyone goes home, it's just the two of you. Spending an excessive amount of money on a wedding extravaganza may become a thing of the past. Inviting people to celebrate your wedding with you was supposed to be a fun thing. It shouldn't take months to prepare for, causing undue stress and anxiety.

I understand we can't put the Genie back into the bottle, considering the hundreds of people employed by the wedding planning industry. But who are you trying to impress with a solo harpist and the releasing of doves?

It's gotten to the point that when calculating the wedding "gift" for the nuptials, you sometimes consider the "cost" of the meal. Does that mean the happy couple that opts for a reasonable wedding gets a smaller "gift" than the couple having their wedding at the Oheka Castle in Huntington? Unfortunately, that's probably true.

With many 2020 wedding celebrations postponed until 2021, couples have decided to forgo the pomp and circumstance to get married anyway. Instead, just a ceremony, followed by a socially distanced dinner with their closest friends and family, will suffice.

My nephew Michael and his fiancé Deirdre are getting married at the end of July. A simple beach wedding in Greenport, followed by a dinner with family and close friends. Like the Rolling Stones sang, "You can't always get what you want. But sometimes, you get what you need." These two kids will start their life together without all the stress, aggravation, and debt, associated with a wedding extravaganza.

Maybe that's not such a bad idea after all...

THE LOSS OF A FURRY FRIEND

2017

We've had the pleasure of sharing our lives with a few dogs over the years. It's not that we are anti-cat, it's just our preference. I had cats as a kid, but my wife is very allergic to them. It wasn't until we became dog owners that I understood the special bond between dogs and their families.

When my friend and his family lost a dear pet, it was the first time in his adult life that he had to experience that type of suffering. I saw the pain and hurt in his eyes when he told me what happened as he reluctantly gained membership into an exclusive club nobody ever wants to join.

Pet owners know the devastating loss of their furry friend. I decided to write this column as a tribute to pets that we have loved and lost.

The Loss of a Furry Friend
By Paul DiSclafani

My friend Bruce and his family recently went through the heartbreaking loss of their furry friend Munchkin, a 15-year-old Bichon Frise. Any long-time pet owner understands the deep bond that develops between a pet and their family. Recognizing that the time you get to share your life with a pet will be brief doesn't make the loss any easier.

I can't speak of the bond families may have with their cat or their turtle, but dogs earned the moniker of "man's best friend" for a reason. Quite frankly, they just are. Like your buddy you go to a ball game with or the bass player in your band, a dog is no less a friend.

They love hanging out with you and will do tricks for you. They speak a completely different language but intuitively know when you're sad or happy. They will follow you anywhere you let them.

Dogs never outgrow that childlike sense of happiness when you come home. Tail wagging, face-licking, and utter joy always greet you when you return. We even talk to dogs like they are humans, even though we know we won't get a verbal response in return. Friends don't need to communicate in words.

Dogs provide something that your human friends seem to be incapable of—unconditional love.

In turn, you love them back. You protect and care for them, rubbing their bellies and scratching the back of their necks. You provide food and shelter, take them to the vet when they are sick. You worry about them.

I've been fortunate enough to have two long-term relationships with dogs. When I was just a teenager, we adopted Sparky, a beagle-sized, mixed-breed companion. He was part of our family for more than 17 years. After marrying and when our boys were old enough, my family welcomed Harry, a Wheaten Terrier. Harry was a member of our family for 16 years.

Both of those dogs were my friends, and losing them was devastating, leaving an unexpected void. Even as a recently married young adult, I remember how distraught I was when we lost Sparky. Later, those same feelings came rushing back when Harry's time was up, only this time I experienced the loss with my grown children. Other than seeing replays of the Mets winning the 1969 World Series, I'm not sure my kids have seen me cry before.

Losing a beloved pet is a traumatic experience, no matter how you slice it. People who love animals can sympathize with your pain, but pet lovers who own pets can feel your pain. Even with the heartbreak of losing your beloved friend, most dog lovers get back into the game at some point in the future. This decision was made for us when my college graduate son returned home with a Labrador named Louie. Of course, like all dogs that have come across my doorstep over the years, my wife is the primary caregiver.

But when my wife isn't around, Louie and I get along like good pals most of the time. We've only known each other for a few years, but I kind of like him. He hangs out with me outside when I smoke a cigar, so he's got that going for him. Our relationship is just beginning.

Human friendships may come and go, but the bond between a dog and his master is for life. Science has proven that companionship with dogs helps us relax, lowers our blood pressure, and keeps us active.

As a consultant over the years, my friend Bruce spent time away from home for days on end. When transitioning between assignments, Munchkin would accompany him on long, solemn walks almost every day. Always by his side and never judgmental, Munchkin was the perfect companion, listening to his jokes and loving every minute of their time together.

When Munchkin passed, I know Bruce and his family lost more than a pet; they lost a member of their family. But I also understand that he lost a good friend.

THE NIGHT THE LIGHTS WENT OUT IN BROOKLYN

2017

On the 40th Anniversary of the 1977 New York City Blackout, I read stories about the chaos that ensued. Long Islanders were spared as this was a Con Edison system issue, affecting only the five boroughs.

Almost 5,000 people were arrested for looting and general mayhem, with 550 police officers injured.

I thought about the first-ever blackout I had experienced as an 8-year-old in Brooklyn back in 1965 and remembered it was more fun than anything. The adults were sitting outside and partying while we kids enjoyed getting to play in the empty streets.

It was a different time, I guess.

The Night the Lights Went out in Brooklyn
By Paul DiSclafani

July 13 marks the 40th anniversary of the blackout that paralyzed New York City in 1977.

On a hot, humid summer evening, a lightning strike at a substation on the Hudson River triggered havoc on the transmission lines. Following a series of mistakes and miscalculations, the entire Con

Edison system shut down, forcing all of New York City into the darkness at 9:36 p.m. We here on Long Island were spared the plunge back into the dark ages thanks to our power company (remember LILCO?) being able to work their magic and keep our lines working.

Many businesses were already closed when complete darkness hit. With people congregating outside to assess the situation, it created a perfect storm for the mayhem that was about to occur. The evening was about to morph into something even darker than New York City without any lights.

More than 4,500 people were arrested during the chaos that ensued, and more than 550 police officers were injured. The NYC Fire department put out 1,037 fires overnight while the citizens held their breath, waiting for daylight to arrive and break the spell. When the dust settled, more than 1,600 businesses had been damaged or destroyed.

Reliving the stories of turmoil during the Blackout of 1977 brought me back to the blackout I experienced as a kid in Brooklyn in November of 1965. Of course, everything that happened "back then" was better, or at least our memories of it are carefully crafted to remember only the good that came of it.

Back then, I took swimming lessons at the YMCA on Tuesday afternoons and would be picked up by a relative, whom I used to call Uncle Nick, around 5:30. My mother and brother would be at my Uncle Joe's house, where we would all meet up for dinner when my father came home.

While driving home with Uncle Nick, we got to a traffic light that wasn't working. It was unusual, but nothing to be alarmed about. Then he noticed all the streetlights were out, and by the time we completed the 10-minute drive, people were starting to mill around in the darkened streets, brandishing candles.

My mother and Aunt Faye, along with every other mother on the block, were in the middle of preparing dinner at 5:27 p.m. when the lights went out. Soon they were on the phone with other relatives, trying to confirm what seemed obvious; the lights were out all over the place.

Crazy talk of an alien attack was cool with us kids but seemed to be frightening the adults. As news reports of the blackout's cause began coming across the battery-operated radios, the initial shock of losing power began to wane.

It seemed power was out in the entire Northeast, but they expected to have it restored in a few hours. This reassuring news changed everything from a worrisome experience into a giddy, after-work gathering. We were way too young to know if alcohol was involved, but you can make your own assumptions.

There was a sense of camaraderie going on, at least in our little section of Brooklyn. Neighbors were sharing candles and helping each other get through the crisis, making the best of the situation. The blackout even sparked a light-hearted movie starring Doris Day called *Where Were You When the Lights Went Out?*

Thirty million people in eight states in the Northeast, roughly 80,000 square miles, were out of power for up to 13 hours. Brooklyn got power back sometime after 11:00 p.m. that night. Most people who faced that blackout think of it fondly as a happening they will never forget.

Many of our parents' generation grew up without a dependency on electricity, so maybe that's why there was no widespread panic. This was their "back then."

That night, across the five boroughs, New York recorded the lowest amount of crime on any night in documented history. Only five people were arrested for looting, and there was no property damage reported. I guess people stayed home and made the best of the situation.

And curiously enough, nine months later, the number of live births was higher than expected...

TIME TO LEAVE THE NEST AND FLY AWAY

2019

Friends of ours were getting ready for their son's move to college. It brought back memories of our first son, James, readying for his journey to East Stroudsburg University in Pennsylvania.

Children going off to college for the first time is a very emotional experience for parents. Their baby is leaving home for the first time.

I remember the weeks leading up to this moment and how I pictured it going. Except none of the versions I saw in my head played out on this day.

This is the true story of his first weekend as an unsupervised adult...

Time to Leave the Nest and Fly
By Paul DiSclafani

It happens every August. The dog days of summer are starting to kick in, and Long Island parents prepare for what many have been dreading since their kids started high school. It's time for little Susie or Johnny to leave the nest and fly off to college.

Unless you have gone through the experience, nothing will prepare you for when you need to leave them on their own for the first time. You thought you had an emotional breakdown the night they had their first sleepover at a friend's house? Baby, you ain't seen nothing yet. Like the first time you became parents, there is no handbook you can refer to when you hug them goodbye, and they head out into life for the first time without you.

Of course, not everyone experiences that Hallmark moment in the same way.

Our firstborn, James, journeyed to East Stroudsburg University in Pennsylvania, just a few miles over the Jersey State line off Route 80. Knowing he was only a few hours away (on a good day) was somehow comforting to us. You know, just in case.

On moving-in day, we packed a rental van with everything he was going to need and headed out for what we assumed would be a very emotional day. Back in 2007, we were required to create a school account we could replenish through our bank linked to his school ID card. That card would be used for everything—access into the dorm, his room, and, more importantly, his daily meals. Just to be sure, we gave him an additional $600 in cash.

That day on campus, we might as well have been invisible. By the time we did all the work and got him set up, he was ready to go off to his new life and seemed anxious to get rid of us. I had prepared myself for a truly emotional farewell, as you see in the movies. Instead, it was more like when you help your friends move into their new home, except there was no pizza and beer at the end of the job.

We had planned to stay in a hotel overnight and take the boys out to breakfast in the morning. Instead, we jumped into the car and drove home. While perusing the paper on Sunday morning to take advantage of an afternoon movie, the phone rang. The caller ID indicated it was James' cell phone.

Uh, oh.

He had been to an off-campus party the night before and lost his wallet, which of course, contained his credit card, his student ID card, and all his cash. What he was doing at an off-campus party on the first night, I can't answer. I didn't ask a lot of questions because, quite frankly, I already knew the answers.

Unfortunately for him, there wasn't anything we could do to bail him out of this mess. He had to wait until Monday to get a new ID card and needed to borrow money from his roommates to get food from the cafeteria. After hanging up the phone, my wife and I looked at each other and shook our heads. When did our kid become such a knucklehead?

We continued to call him each week to find out how things were going, but sometime before Thanksgiving, he phoned to say he found the wallet.

"The girl that hosted the party found it," he said so triumphantly. "It was inside the pocket of a pair of jeans she found in her drawer and still had the $600 in it."

At that point, I decided I didn't want to know anything more about it. Turns out we were prepared for James to leave the nest, but he wasn't ready to fly.

UNDERSTANDING THE SACRIFICES OF OUR VETERANS

2018

Earlier in this collection, you read the story about my Uncle Sammy, a hero in World War II.

In 2018, my family got together to have his name added to Nassau County's "Walls of Honor" at Eisenhower Park. It's a yearly ceremony dedicated to honoring those who served in the military, living or dead. Part of the ceremony is the unveiling of the new engravings on the wall. For a $100 donation, anyone that served in the military will be honored.

I have never attended a ceremony that was so moving. To see, firsthand, the veterans who participated in the ceremonies and their physical struggles were overwhelming. The men and women who served in our country's military to defend our way of life and protect us are real-life heroes.

Today, it seems so easy to reach out to them and thank them for their service. But in reality, it's no more than shaking hands and telling them to have a nice day. It's a nice gesture that allows us to recognize and respect our veterans, but can we ever truly understand their sacrifice?

I decided to do the next best thing and dedicated one of my columns to these veterans.

Later that same year, I organized a massive initiative within my family to honor all our fathers who served to have their names engraved on the Walls of Honor in time for the 2019 ceremony. I coordinated with my cousins and other relatives, collected their paperwork (and individual checks), and sent a giant package to the Nassau County Veterans Monument Fund (11 engravings in all). By sending one package before the 12/31/2018 deadline, our relatives were assured of being engraved on the wall together.

Sometime in February, I received a call from someone representing the Monument Fund. Although there was no problem with our applications, she wanted to talk to me personally and thank me.

Thank me?

She told me they were sent a copy of this column after it was published. They were very moved and have been including it in every return package sent out to people who request engravings.

Although I never served in the military, my father was a veteran of the Korean War. He sacrificed being away from his family while spending time in Germany, Italy, and France. Due to his brother's ultimate sacrifice (my Uncle Sammy), he never had to see action on the front lines. Immediately following his return from active duty, he married my mother.

For some who made the ultimate sacrifice, they didn't get a happy reunion. For the others, they carry those sacrifices for the rest of their lives.

Understanding the Sacrifices of Our Veterans
By Paul DiSclafani

We see and hear every day about supporting those who serve in the military. It's the one cause that unites both Democrats and Republicans. Throughout our history, this country has been defined by wars and the bloodshed by soldiers performing their duty. All those sacrifices so we could enjoy the freedoms we take for granted every day.

Not every member of the service made the ultimate sacrifice, but their sacrifices were still significant. The "Walls of Honor," located at Eisenhower Park just outside the BandShell, is a series of tributes and monuments dedicated to those brave men and women.

For a $100 donation, any service member's name (from any conflict) will be added to stainless-steel panels mounted on granite monuments. With the names of soldiers as far back as the War of

1812, these monuments commemorate our military members (living or dead) who served this nation through its darkest moments or protected it in times of peace.

This year's "unveiling" ceremony on June 23 drew well over 2,000 people celebrating our veterans' achievements, adding more than 300 names to the monuments, now honoring over 10,000 service members. Although most public ceremonies are usually filled with politicians getting a photo opportunity, this was different. There were no politics on display this afternoon, only a sense of pride while being surrounded by true Patriots.

With a crowd full of veterans wearing uniforms or other identifying garments, you got a true feeling of what this was all about. The veterans took the spotlight, delivering heartfelt speeches and giving the crowd a sense of the real sacrifices they chose to make. But if you ask them, there's not a hero among them.

Somehow, standing and reciting the Pledge of Allegiance and "Star Spangled Banner" took on a different significance. It wasn't just a run-through, so we can get to the next stage of the ceremony or start the ball game. It felt different and had meaning to everyone there. I've recited that pledge and stood for the anthem thousands of times in my life, but not like this, and not amongst veterans struggling to escape wheelchairs while leaning on friends and family to participate with honor.

Veterans from all conflicts share that common sacrifice, and their discussion led to a common theme. Their concern is that future generations will not remember.

Nick Graziano is Chairman of the Nassau County Veterans Memorial Fund, which is responsible for the monuments. The Vietnam veteran spoke passionately about ensuring teachers do a better job of educating students about what happened during these conflicts.

"Educators are not telling the real stories of war," he said, adding, "Remind them how we saved the world, not once, but twice."

He also implored veterans to talk to their children about their service and sacrifice. "Make sure you tell your children about what this means," he said, "Remember, reflection and pay tribute to those we lost and those who served."

"I was killed in Vietnam," Graziano said, "But I just didn't die yet. Some came home with ticking time bombs in their bodies, some came home under a flag, and others never came home." He also reminded us what General George Patton said of soldiers making the ultimate sacrifice. "It is foolish and wrong to mourn the men who died. Rather we should thank God that such men lived."

92-year-old veteran Angel Ciotta, a survivor of Iwo Jima, was honored for his contributions to all the memorials at Eisenhower. He was barely 18 when he landed on the beach at Iwo Jima. "Whatever you are enjoying today did not come free," he said, "It was paid for in blood, sweat, and death. We left white crosses all over the world."

As the ceremonies wound down, it was almost time for everyone to turn their attention to the monuments and locate their loved one's name. In honor of those lost, there was a jolting 21-gun salute, followed by the haunting playing of "Taps," while the crowd bowed their heads and many wept silently.

OH MY! I HAVE ONYCHOPHAGIA

2018

I like to be honest with my readers, often discussing events in my life. I'm also not shy about revealing my human frailties. I make mistakes, run into trouble every now and then, and have bad habits. The life of a columnist is sometimes an open book.

If you don't know what onychophagia is (pronounced **Ahh-Ne-Ko-Fay-Gee-Ahh**)*, you will when you read this next piece.*

I suffer from it.

Who knows? Maybe you suffer from it and never even knew it?

Oh My! I Have Onychophagia
By Paul DiSclafani

Recently, our niece's four-year-old asked me, rather innocently, what was wrong with my finger? Although I had no injury, she pointed to the index finger on my left hand, which was raw and red. I immediately understood what her concern was.

You see, I bite my fingernails.

I guess I never gave it a second thought, just something I've always done. I can go long periods without biting them (I do own nail clippers, you know), but to be honest with you, I don't pay that much attention to it. Of all the terrible things you could do to your body, this is probably way down on the list.

An "oral parafunctional habit" is defined as using the mouth for a purpose other than speaking, eating, or drinking. This includes grinding your teeth, sucking your fingers, pencil chewing, or mouth breathing. Geeze, I'm guilty of all those things from time to time. I'm still opening bags of chips with my teeth. According to medical journals, it starts during childhood, increases during adolescence, and declines with age.

Except, mine never went away. As a child, I never had a pacifier (although both my kids had "nookies"), and I never sucked my thumb. But I can't ever remember not biting my nails. It's one thing to exhibit specific behavior; it's quite another to find out there is an actual name for it.

"Nail-biting" is considered temporary and non-destructive. Still, after 50 years, it's regarded as a "pathological oral habit and grooming disorder." That doesn't sound good at all. As a matter of fact, it even has a name: Onychophagia. Oh my, I'm not even sure I can pronounce that.

Here, I thought it was just a disgusting habit, like smoking, except it doesn't lead to lung cancer. Now I find out I've been categorized, along with other body-focused repetitive behavior disorders (BFRBDs). When you're categorized and assigned a "definition," that's heavy stuff. Now there are symptoms, causes, and even treatments.

In the old days, they coated the kid's fingers in a bitter-tasting substance to prevent nail-biting. I've never tried that, but then again, I never knew I had an actual medical condition.

I had no idea it was considered obsessive-compulsive behavior. People mostly bite their nails during stressful times. Sports announcers even call tight games "nail biters." Biters usually do it because they are bored, nervous, lonely, or hungry. I'm not sure what category I fall into, but ever since I heard of onychophagia, I noticed how often I bite my nails.

Quite frankly, it's frightening!

Like anyone, I've had instances where a nail broke, and I had to do a quick oral "repair"—who hasn't? You're not allowed to bring nail clippers on an airplane anymore, you know. What more stressful situation are you going to get than that?

My wife has reprimanded me a few times when catching me biting my nails, mostly while I'm driving. Again, I seem to find myself doing it while watching television or at my desk. Most of the time, I'm not even paying attention.

I've never pulled my own hair or purposely cut my skin, or done any of those other BFRBD types of behaviors, so I don't see a straitjacket in my future. I just have a terrible habit of biting my nails. I wonder if they have group therapy sessions for people with onychophagia, you know, like Onychophagia Anonymous? They might meet in some church basement twice a month, serving coffee and doughnuts.

"My name is Paul DiSclafani, and I have Ahh-Ne-Ko-Fay-Gee-Ahh..."

If you see me in a work meeting or on a plane absentmindedly chomping on a cuticle, have mercy on me. I guess I'll be alright.

I just hope I don't find out there's a medical condition for picking your nose...

THE MYSTERY OF AUGUST 14TH, 2003

2018

There is a reason why the TV show <u>The Twilight Zone</u> was so popular. Most people have experienced things during their lives that just cannot be explained. This is the true story of what happened to us on August 14th, 2003.

Due to size limitations in the printed version, this story appeared over two parts in consecutive weeks in the <u>Massapequa Observer</u>. I've taken the liberty of combining it into one story for this collection.

Since I don't want to spoil anything for you, dear readers, I'd like my good friend Rod Sterling to provide the introduction:

Imagine, if you will, a time when we were still gripped by the events of September 11th, 2001. A time when uncertainty reigned high and terror was still on everyone's mind. A family amid a pilgrimage, if you will, to the Baseball Hall of Fame in the tony town of Cooperstown, New York, a place that has remained untouched from its roots almost a century ago. Now imagine that family coming to grips with a developing crisis around them as their only form of escape was slowly draining the life out of them. Imagine an oasis, if you will, rising out of the desert sand to give them hope. An oasis that could be found only, in The Twilight Zone...

The Mystery of August 14th, 2003
By Paul DiSclafani

We had finally arrived. After more than 40 minutes of winding, twisting, rural roads dotted with farmland and forests, we approached Cooperstown in upstate New York. It was quite a difference once we turned off Interstate 88, leaving civilization behind and being transported into a seemingly different era in time.

Although the calendar said August 14th, 2003, our surroundings indicated something out of the 1950s, only everything wasn't in black-and-white. We pulled our converted Chevy Astro-Van into the Park-and-Ride lot just outside of town, completing the journey with a ride on the retro-looking trolley. The ride only took a few minutes, but the closer we got to the middle of town, the more we realized that this travel mode was the only way to go.

There were no giant parking lots and certainly no parking available on the main or side streets. No, this was a town designed for strolling down the tree-lined sidewalks in a land that time forgot.

The National Baseball Hall of Fame is the main attraction in Cooperstown, our destination on this beautiful, hot August afternoon. After four-plus hours in the car on the way up here, we needed to refuel and stopped for lunch.

Just down the block stood the air-conditioned Hall of Fame, where we spent a reasonable amount of time. With my wife and teenage son James in tow, we perused the different colorful, informative, and interactive exhibits. The museum tour ends in the Great Hall, a solemn place where bronze plaques are displayed, commemorating the great, enshrined players.

Suddenly, the air-conditioning in the Great Hall shut off, and the emergency lights came on. The Great Hall had lost power and was rapidly turning into the Great Sauna. It was almost 4:30 p.m. now, and after spending a few hours in the museum, we decided to head to the souvenir shop in the lobby. Regrettably, without power, the cash registers weren't working.

Once out in the street, it became apparent the entire block was powerless. Merchants and patrons dotted the storefronts and streets with befuddled looks on their faces. Surrounded by confusion, we decided to head home.

Waiting on the line for the Park-and-Ride trolley with the other weary travelers, James overheard people talking about the power outage, indicating all of New York was out of power. Being just two years removed from the World Trade Center's terror attacks, I could see the concern on his face. I explained that since the last major blackout, measures were put in place to protect the power grid and contain the outage. I couldn't have been more wrong.

Back at the van, the disturbing news on the radio confirmed the entire Northeast was indeed out of power. Since we couldn't do much about it, we piled into the van and considered getting a room for the night in Cooperstown, hoping to find a vacancy along the way out of town. If not, we had about a four-hour trip ahead of us, and things might get sorted out by the time we got back to Long Island.

Heading out, I remembered that we needed gas, so I pulled into the nearest station. Unfortunately, without electricity, they had no way of pumping gas. I went to the next station and the one after that, all with the same problem; electric pumps require electricity. To add insult to injury, we passed several motels, soon realizing there were no vacancies in Cooperstown.

Beginning our trek home with the gas gauge firmly on "E," I tried to remain calm and not alarm anyone (like my wife). Suddenly, the winding, twisting, rural road back to the Interstate that was so charming on the way here was now worrisome and terrifying.

Although I was sure the Interstate gas stations would have generator power, we weren't going to make it that far…

Unfortunately, my gas gauge was already on "E," and we needed to find a station that could pump gas without electricity. Trying to calculate how many miles I might be able to go past the "E," I was hoping the urban legend was true, and there really was still gas left in the tank.

There is nothing more harrowing than driving on a lonely, winding road with only farms as far as the eye can see, in a vehicle about to run out of fuel. If my memory serves me, it was at least 40 minutes before we got to Interstate 88. What was I going to do when we started to sputter on our last fumes?

I thought about pulling into a farm, hoping they might use a manual pump to fuel their farm vehicles. If not, we could always sleep in the Astro-Van, since it was equipped for comfort.

With the gas gauge slipping below "E," we were still in the middle of nowhere. My wife, now aware of the situation, kept up a brave front as our remaining gas withered away. We continued passing farm after farm before a few small businesses began showing up.

In a clearing ahead, I spied a run-down, roadside motel that reminded me of every horror movie I've ever seen. Without any type of "vacancy" sign, I made an executive decision to give it a try. It was still daylight, and at least we had a parking lot to use overnight if we had to sleep in the van.

A stereotypical motel clerk emerged from the back to greet us, and to my relief, told us there was a room available. Talk about being lucky! There may have been no electricity for air conditioning, but it certainly had to be better than sleeping in the van.

She slid the required paperwork across the counter. When I reached for the pen, the paperwork flew off the counter and onto the floor. Without thinking, I retrieved it and began filling in the blanks. Curiously, the edges of the paper were moving up and down as I continued to write. I instinctively glanced up and noticed the breeze from the ceiling fan was causing the paper to move.

This motel had power!

The clerk explained there were about four blocks, for some reason, that still had power, including the Stewart's on the corner, where we could get a sandwich. More importantly, they were still pumping gas.

After checking into our room, which under normal circumstances would have caused us to run screaming from, I took the van down the block to Stewart's to gas up. I returned with food, drinks, and two cans of bug spray. Since the room had air conditioning and electricity, we ignored the now dead insects and watched the confusion unfolding back home on TV. By morning, order and electricity had been restored to the universe, and we continued our journey home.

Retelling the story, my brother asked what town we found the mystery motel in. To be honest, I didn't remember. We tried to locate the town on a map but couldn't find it. Oddly, I had no receipt from either the motel or Stewart's, and I saved every receipt. It was as if the entire thing didn't happen.

It's a mystery that we've never been able to solve, even with the satellite images available today on Google Maps. Maybe on the next trip to Cooperstown, we'll pass that Mystery Motel.

One thing's for sure, I'll have plenty of gas.

WHERE IS MY WIFE?

2018

My wife is not usually a "spur of the moment" type of person. Don't get me wrong, she likes to do some things spontaneously but not something as extravagant as this, especially when it revolves around a sporting event.

I've been blessed to be in a relationship with someone who is understanding of my sports fanaticism. I've had plenty of "spur of the moment" incidents where friends have gotten me tickets to ballgames at the last minute and have never been denied my passion.

But this? This was something completely different.

Where is My Wife?
By Paul DiSclafani

I'm not sure, but I think my wife has been replaced by a cyborg.

Not that there's anything wrong with cyborgs, but this replica is way too close for comfort to the real thing. She looks the same and talks the same. She dresses like my wife and even goes to the barn to take care of Stormy, her horse. She still takes care of the house, walks Louie, and makes meals for everyone. No, this cyborg had perfected my wife's mannerisms and idiosyncrasies. However, it made a simple, fatal mistake almost any sports fan would recognize immediately, especially a husband.

Last week on a Tuesday, she casually asked what we should do with the upcoming weekend, suggesting we invite friends or catch a movie. Although I usually agree with either of those two plans, I was watching the ballgame at the time and kiddingly responded with a ridiculous notion.

"I'd like to go to Boston and see the Mets play at Fenway Park on Saturday," I answered. Now I just waited, knowing full well the response would be met with an eye-roll and a light-hearted sarcastic remark.

But to my utter surprise, she simply said, "Book it. Let's go."

Excuse me?

I thought for sure my plan would be met with resistance, or at least a "What are you, insane?" I even had a whole spiel planned to play up the cultural aspects of the trip, ending with, "Then we could go to the game…" But I didn't have to sell it at all.

You know the old saying, "opposites attract"? When it comes to a love for sports, there are no more opposites on the planet than my wife and me. Don't get me wrong, during 35 years of marriage, she's been a real trooper, accompanying me to many ballgames. But it's just not her thing, you know? Getting there for the first pitch and staying for the last out is not a priority for her. And there is nothing that will ruin her day, like the dreaded words, "We're going into extra innings."

I cautioned that although I could cancel the hotel room, I couldn't get my money back on the game tickets.

She simply said, "I told you to book it, so book it." She even wanted to borrow a Mets shirt from one of the kids.

Who is this person?

So, I did what any utterly perplexed husband would do when his wife agrees with a completely ridiculous idea. I booked a trip to Boston before she could change her mind.

As Saturday approached, I wondered if there was some other nefarious reason for her agreeing to this hair-brained scheme without even hearing the details (or the projected cost). Was she going to use this against me down the road and guilt me into doing something that I would usually never agree to? Although I jumped all over this wonderful opportunity to spend the weekend with my wife and go to Fenway Park for the first time, I was a little apprehensive. My initial thought was that this couldn't possibly be my wife, but whomever this person turns out to be, I wasn't going to pass up this opportunity.

Well, we had a lovely weekend.

Turns out there was a group of over 1,600 Mets fans, from the "7-Line Army," assembling across the street from our hotel to walk parade-style through the streets of Boston to Fenway Park. We joined the group taking over the streets and chanting "Let's Go Mets," and my wife (or this reasonable facsimile) was louder than me at times. Although the Mets lost, we stayed for the entire game without any hint of leaving before the final out.

So, what do I do now? I know this can't possibly be my wife, but is that such a bad thing?

When we got home on Sunday, we were heading back out for an afternoon of music to see the band "Bad Sandwich" with some friends. Just then my wife-like cyborg said, "If you want to stay home and watch football, that's OK."

Now I know something's not right, but who am I to rock the boat?

THE SCOURGE OF LONG ISLAND: THE CAVE CRICKET

2017

I don't like bugs, never have.

I wrote this column out of pure terror from experiencing Cave Crickets up close and personal for the first time. I'd heard about them and had been warned, but there is nothing like coming face-to-face with the little buggers.

When I began writing this column regularly in the Spring of 2017, I was still finding my voice. I started to connect with the readers and became more popular as the weeks went along. I must have hit a nerve with this column.

The response was instantaneous. To date, it is still the most popular column I have ever written. I still get emails when someone finds it in my catalog. It's been shared on multiple platforms and was one of the most commented on items I have ever posted on Facebook.

Seems I'm not alone in my utter disgust for these creatures.

The Scourge of Long Island: The Cave Cricket
By Paul DiSclafani

Full disclosure—I am "bug-a-phobic." I detest all bugs and have no tolerance for them. I am a "shoot first and ask questions later" type of person when it comes to bugs. "See them, squash them," that's my credo.

I don't think I could ever live in Florida or the Carolinas because I've seen the Palmetto bug up close and personal, and it's not a pretty sight. There isn't much you can do when giant cockroaches come up out of your shower drain, is there? I've thought about Arizona, but they have scorpions hiding in your boots. No, thank you. I don't need to live someplace where bugs can kill you.

As a kid, I was once traumatized by a Praying Mantis in the ultra-back of my father's station wagon while visiting relatives in Howard Beach. To this day, I can still see its silhouette in the dark as it sat on my knee. Oh, the horror! And don't get me started on Brooklyn roaches.

Another Summer staple in these parts is the buzzing cicada, which terrifies me to the point of running away like a 10-year-old girl. But we have mutual respect for each other—I leave them alone, and they don't land on my head.

However, there is a new scourge of bugs here on Long Island that is wreaking havoc and chaos—the cave cricket. Some call them "camel" or "spider" crickets, but you can call them what you want. These things are the spawn of the devil.

I first heard about them from friends living in Bellmore. They must be migrating east because they began appearing here in Massapequa a few years ago, infiltrating my shed and then my basement. Quite frankly, I am frightened of them. They are huge, prehistoric-looking things with long legs and tentacles. I would recommend you google them, but I don't want to be responsible for your future nightmares. They have a mouth and can gnaw at just about anything, including clothing, plants, and other insects.

They don't have sharp, pointy teeth like the killer rabbit in *Monty Python and The Holy Grail*, so they really can't harm you in any physical way. However, when you open your shed to get something, there is no way to prepare for giant crickets leaping at you from different directions. These crickets have such powerful hind legs; they can vault over your head. Jumping is their only defense mechanism, and it's used to scare off predators.

Mission accomplished.

Imagine watching a bad horror movie in 3D as things come at you from all directions. The only recourse you have is to cover your face and scream. Not only do cave crickets jump, but they also jump sideways. They are lightning-fast, springing at you immediately upon sensing your presence, not waiting for you to gather your courage and secure a weapon, like a broom.

There seem to be only two options for controlling these creatures—glue traps and bug bombs. The problem with glue traps is that once these monsters get stuck on them, they will gnaw their own legs off to escape.

Do you see the type of terror we are dealing with?

And if they can't escape, other cave crickets will attempt to cannibalize their body for food. Am I painting a clear enough picture here? Just the thought of picking up a glue trap covered with these creatures gives me the willies.

Unfortunately, the only choice seems to be the nuclear option, the bug bomb. I could tolerate them in my shed, although now I wear hockey goalie equipment when I get a rake, but not in my house. That is my fortress of solitude, and I will not put up with jumping intruders lurking in my laundry room.

I have secured the necessary weapons of mass destruction and confirmed the nuclear codes. Soon my basement will be engulfed in a fog of chemicals designed to eradicate the enemy with minimal property damage. Tomorrow, I will bravely survey ground zero and perform a visual inspection to ensure the threat has been neutralized.

Of course, I'll have to use a remote drone camera since there is no way I am ever going downstairs into my laundry room again.

WELCOME TO THE FAMILY

2019

I like to share details of my life with my readers, and this was such a happy occasion, I couldn't resist.

Welcome to the Family
By Paul DiSclafani

Our baby is getting married.

Kevin, our youngest son, and his longtime girlfriend Arielle are officially fiancés. We learned of the happy news recently and are ready to welcome a new member to the family, joining James, Louie the Labrador, and Stormy the horse.

Kevin had alerted me to the coming proposal earlier when he ominously came into my home office with a strange look on his face, mumbling, "I did something today."

Uh oh.

I wasn't sure what words were coming out his mouth next but anticipated something along the lines of, "I crashed my car," "I quit my job," or, just fill in the blank with a horrible thought. I was taken aback when he showed me the little box with an engagement ring inside.

He indicated he was going to pop the question in a few weeks when they went on vacation. I guess he couldn't wait.

Kevin and Arielle have been like two peas in a pod for a long time now. They enjoy sports and are both big Mets fans. They've traveled to see the Mets play in places like San Diego and Pittsburgh, to name a few. On vacation, they enjoy attending sporting events, taking in NFL and NHL games in Tennessee, some of the World Cup Hockey games in Toronto, and even non-Mets baseball games in Boston. These kids are so in love and do so many things together. Quite frankly, it makes me sick (just kidding).

So, I guess it was no surprise that Kevin called me from the Mets game at Citi Field against Washington that he and Arielle were attending. It was a surprise when he told me he had proposed to Arielle just before they went into the stadium.

Even though I knew it was coming sometime very shortly, it hit me hard. My Kevin, who will always be eight years old in my eyes, had decided to take that next step.

Just then, a huge roar came from the crowd all around him as one of the Mets had just hit a game-tying home run. It was almost poetic. Although the proposal wasn't anything corny, like having it done on the scoreboard in front of 40,000 people. It was unique, nonetheless. It combined their love for each other with their passion for sports.

When Citi Field first opened, they were selling commemorative "bricks" to be installed outside the stadium. The bricks could be customized with a special message that would live in perpetuity, something you could visit each time you went to the ballpark for generations. As huge Mets fans, we bought a brick and inscribed it with something other than "Let's Go Mets," which you could read on 80 percent of the others.

Instead, I went with something 1986 World Series hero Mookie Wilson once told me while signing autographs for the kids at a scouting event when they were little. Mookie hit the ball that went trickling through Bill Buckner's legs in Game 6 of that magical year, allowing the Mets to complete an improbable comeback. He told me that even if Buckner had caught that ball, he would have beaten him to the base and been safe. Thus, the engraving says, "Mookie Would Have Beaten It—DISCLAFANI 2010."

Kevin covertly led Arielle to our family brick, near the Tom Seaver entrance. In front of their friends (who were in on what was about to happen) and any strangers watching, he got down on one knee and proposed. How romantic was that?

Here's to two kids who are beginning their lives together, taking a leap of faith, just like all of us did at some point.

Wait, this means I must get ready for a wedding soon. Anyone know the number for Jenny Craig?

THERE IS CRYING IN BASEBALL

2020

Kids who grew up as sports fans always had their favorite players.

Even Charlie Brown had a favorite baseball player, Joe Shlabotnik. Unfortunately, while other kids watched their heroes hit home runs and win games for their team, Shlabotnik was being sent down to the minors.

Tom Seaver was my favorite ballplayer. He passed away in August of 2020. For some reason, that really stung me. As a kid, some of my best memories were watching Seaver drag the Mets kicking and screaming out of the basement and into respectability. The Mets were no longer the laughing stock of baseball, thanks to Seaver.

He had disappeared from the public back in 2019 due to his battles with Alzheimer's and Lyme Disease. But the passing of the man who was dubbed "The Franchise" hit me when I least expected.

I had heard about his death while perusing my Facebook feed and immediately turned to the Mets TV partner, SNY, to confirm. Sure enough, he was gone.

I watched the coverage and listened to all the guests talk about how great a person he was and wax poetic about his greatness as a baseball player. He was a Hall of Famer, after all. On my last trip to Baseball's Hall of Fame in Cooperstown, I got a chance to view his plaque in The Great Hall and was overcome with both pride and emotion. There, sharing space with the greatest players in the history of baseball, was my favorite baseball player. Seaver was the first player from the Mets to be inducted into the Hall.

As I stood and read his plaque, like a proud poppa, I was overcome with emotion. Embarrassed by my reaction, I tried to covertly wipe the tears escaping down my cheek. I noticed several other fans, some much older than me, having the same response as they stood before their favorite players' plaques.

It was one thing to watch former players and reporters talking about Seaver's storied career. Still, it was another thing when they started showing the video of him as a 25-year-old. That's when I was flooded with emotions as I was instantly transported back to being that 12-year-old kid watching ball games with my father. He had seen some of the greatest ball players of all time play, but told me how special Seaver was.

I couldn't let his passing go by without my own personal tribute.

This column helped "Long Island Living" win First Place for the category "Narrative-Column" in the 2021 Press Club of Long Island Media Awards.

There is Crying in Baseball
By Paul DiSclafani

Tom Seaver passed away.

He was more than just a baseball player to a generation of Mets fans. He was the best baseball player, and he was ours. He was young, brash, talented, and good-looking. He even had a beautiful, blonde wife. To a 12-year-old kid, he was a hero without a cape.

Should athletes be looked up to and revered by young kids? If they were all like Tom Seaver, the answer was a resounding yes.

When I saw the story of his passing on my Facebook feed, I was sad but not surprised. Last year, Seaver retired from "public" life due to his struggles with dementia. His pride would not allow him to be seen in a compromising position. Seaver also battled Lyme disease for a long time. He was 75 when he died.

It wasn't until I turned to the Mets sports channel, SNY, and saw the vibrant 25-year-old Seaver again, that I realized I was weeping. I became that 12-year-old kid again, living and dying with the 1969 Mets. I was back in the schoolyard, playing ball with my friends and all we could talk about was baseball and the Mets. I was suddenly watching a baseball game again with my father. Huddled around our black-and-white TV, we watched in horror as Jimmy Qualls dropped a base hit off Seaver with one out in the ninth inning, ruining his bid for a perfect game. I still remember howling with disgust, causing my mother to admonish us for being so emotional over a "stupid" baseball game.

Did Tom Seaver have any direct effect on my life? Other than trying to emulate his iconic delivery off the mound every time I threw a pitch in Wiffle Ball, no. You didn't live your life to "be" Tom Seaver, but you certainly had a Mets shirt with his number on it.

I read somewhere that there are a few signs of getting older that men begin to notice as they age. First, the playboy centerfolds are younger than you. The others revolve around your sports heroes as they progress through their careers. They retire, then get elected into the Hall of Fame and finally get their number retired. Of course, they eventually die.

Tom Seaver was my first sports hero, and you always remember your first. The fact that he was one of the greatest pitchers of all time was a bonus but not the reason he was my hero. After years of futility as the "lovable loser" Mets, Seaver was not having any of that. He wasn't happy just being a part of the Mets. Seaver wanted the Mets to be winners, just like the fans did. He led by example in his preparation, his performance, and, of course, his results.

There's a great scene in the baseball movie *The Sandlot* where one of the kids has a dream about being visited by Babe Ruth. Ruth told him, "Heroes get remembered, but legends never die." I'll never forget what Tom Seaver meant to me as a kid growing up, and his legendary status as one of the greatest baseball players will never die.

The ironic thing is that just last week, I needed to change my password at work. You can never reuse a password, so trying to come up with something unique every 90 days or so is getting more difficult for old-timers like me. I had just changed it to "Seaver41". It wasn't until I went to log on this morning that I realized how difficult it was to type that password. So, I immediately changed it to honor my baseball hero.

Now, like his uniform number, my Seaver41 password has been retired.

ANOTHER SUMMER HAS COME AND GONE

2018

I thought about how great summer was as a kid. Although adults also love summer, we are always concerned about "wasting" those special days. Summer means different things to kids and adults.

I used this column to explore those differences.

Another Summer Has Come and Gone
By Paul DiSclafani

One of the saddest parts of late August is looking outside and realizing it's starting to get dark before 8:00 p.m. Remember that feeling of euphoria in the early spring when sunlight was still lingering around dinner time? After a winter of seemingly endless darkness, the gradual extension of daylight was almost imperceptible. Then one day, you get home from work, and you can still catch the sunset.

As kids, we looked forward to summer because it liberated us from homework and classes. There were bicycles to ride, baseball games to play, pools to swim in, and hanging outside late with your friends—under the streetlight, of course. I don't think I used a pencil all summer, except to keep score at a ballgame.

AM radio was the soundtrack to our lives during the summer, repeating hits over and over. Even today, hearing certain songs takes you back to those hot, humid nights that we hoped would never end.

Back then, there were no concerns over wasting a summer. That's what summers were for—to be wasted. No obligations, no responsibilities. As adults, rainy days might ruin your plans, but they sent us indoors for board games and bad horror movies on TV. We'd imagine ourselves as superheroes fighting bad guys or Captain Kirk commanding the Starship Enterprise. There was an unlimited number of diversions from the nothingness that is summer for a kid.

But as an adult, summer takes on a different meaning.

Unless you're a teacher, July might as well be November because you still have to go to work. But during the summer, we adults seem to obsess over "doing something." Whereas kids view the coming of September as an impending doom interrupting their good time, adults look at the coming of September to reflect on how much of the summer they wasted.

"Why didn't we have more barbecues and enjoy our backyard?"

"How come we didn't spend more time at the beach?"

"I never went on one bicycle ride or walked the boardwalk."

"Are the free summer concerts over?"

Most of us have participated in more adult summers than kid summers. Several factors work against us thoroughly enjoying those precious 92 days. For one thing, the unrelenting march of time for an adult seems to speed up as you get older. Sometimes, there aren't enough hours in a day. You still come home from work on a Tuesday to prepare dinner. The house needs to be cleaned, and laundry needs to be done. The only real difference is that it's still daylight when you start to wind down at 8:00 p.m.

Granted, there are weekday evenings you have an activity planned, but those are few and far between. Most of the time, your "get-up-and-go" just "got-up-and-went." One of the summer's nicest perks is the weather being pleasant enough to enjoy the twilight in your backyard. Unless, of course, you actually try to enjoy the twilight in your backyard. You quickly learn twilight happens to coincide with dinnertime for mosquitos.

As another summer slowly dwindles, we should look back at some of the fun we did have. We vacationed in New England, went to a free concert or two, and, like everyone else on Long Island, lost many battles with the mosquitos. We had the occasional dinner with friends and did some swimming. I read a few books, smoked a few good cigars, and gained more weight than I'd like to admit.

None of us really know how many more summers we have left, so I guess we really don't want to waste them. But as kids, we were never concerned with wasting the summer. We just did what we wanted to do, and nobody kept score. I stopped keeping score a long time ago, so I'm never disappointed.

Thanks for everything, Summer of 2018. I'll keep my fingers crossed that we all get through this coming winter together and look forward to noticing when the days start getting longer again.

WHERE EVERYBODY KNOWS YOUR NAME

2019

This column was part of the package submitted that helped <u>Long Island Living</u> take Second Place in the 2020 Press Club of Long Island Media Awards in the "Narrative-Column" category.

It just so happened the location of the dentist office was the same building as my old "watering hole," a place called Jocelyn's. Oh, the memories that came flooding back when I first stepped into the office. I knew every inch of that building like the back of my hand.

While making small talk with the dental hygienist, I told her how familiar I was with the building and regaled her with a few tales from my past in Jocelyn's.

Unfortunately for me, my memories of the history behind the building weren't as sharp as I thought...

Where Everybody Knows Your Name
By Paul DiSclafani

Have you ever had an utterly harmless discussion turn out to be one of your most embarrassing moments?

Growing up as part of the bar scene in the late '70s, we spent plenty of evenings visiting different places to take advantage of drink specials or great cover bands. We also had a "Home Base" that served us well. "Jocelyn's" on Merrick Road in Massapequa was our place, where everyone knew your name, and you knew everyone's name. It was our home away from home. As frequent visitors, we were more than just patrons; we were family. Forty years later, I've been blessed to still call most of them my friends.

But life marches on. Once we moved from college into married life, we remained friends but frequented "Jocelyn's" less and less. When we learned the closing was inevitable, it was just another part of our lives that we had to leave behind.

Fast forward to ten years later.

Needing a new dentist, I decided to give my wife's current one, Dr. DeFeo, a try. Although I was never a patient there, I was very familiar with the location. You guessed it, they took over and renovated the building previously occupied by "Jocelyn's."

It was kind of surreal to walk into that shoe-box-shaped building after all these years and find it was now a dental office. There were no signs of it ever being my favorite watering hole, except for the front door placement. Once inside, though, I knew precisely where everything used to be.

I was led into one of the small treatment rooms located in the back, where the Foosball table and bowling machine once collected our hard-earned quarters. Making small talk with the young hygienist, I told her what a strange experience this was for me, regaling her with my memories of the old "Jocelyn's." I pointed out where the stage was located and how the bar was against the wall, where the receptionist was now. I even admitted to spending many evenings in this building. Yes, I told her of all the great, great memories and friendships I had made there.

But something didn't feel right. Although I didn't expect the hygienist to understand what it meant to me as I reminisced about my old stomping ground, she seemed more surprised than entertained. I shrugged it off and never gave it a second thought.

When I got home, I told my wife how weird it was to go back into the old building. I told her of the conversations I had with the hygienist and the staff, mentioning they seemed a little taken aback at my reminiscing.

That's when she reminded me. After Jocelyn's closed, it reopened as a topless joint.

Of course, I had forgotten!

A giggle joint called The Class Act took over the building for a few years. The dental office staff knew nothing about my beloved Jocelyn's because the previous tenant was a topless joint!

Oh, my goodness, what they must have thought!

Here I was innocently telling them about all the time I spent there, how it was my favorite place, and knowing everyone there. Yet all they saw was a degenerate spending every evening at a topless joint! Oh, the horror!

When I arrived for my appointment the following week, I was greeted with more recognition and smiles than a second-time patient deserved. Getting settled in the chair, I immediately told that same hygienist about the terrible misunderstanding regarding my statements from last week. I explained that I was talking about Jocelyn's, not The Class Act. She seemed to understand, and we all had a good laugh about it.

Just like when I was a regular at Jocelyn's, everyone still knows my name in this building. Only this time, it was for all the wrong reasons.

ENOUGH ALREADY WITH PUMPKIN SPICE

2017

Although Pumpkin Pie is a staple at most Thanksgiving Feasts, it is my least favorite pie. I would make sure to sample every other possible dessert and then make an excuse for not "trying" the Pumpkin Pie. Let's be honest, at the end of the day, which pie on your table had the most still left in the pan?

Around 2010, micro-breweries began making Pumpkin Spice beer.

By the time I sat down to write this column in 2017, the dreaded pumpkin spice was being infused in just about every edible product known to man. I decided to have some fun with it, and this was the result.

Enough Already with Pumpkin Spice
By Paul DiSclafani

Some time ago, a friend of mine took me to John Harvard's in Smithtown. She was excited because it was time for their special brew, a pumpkin spice beer, which would only be available for a few weeks each fall. Once the calendar turned to December, it would be gone until next year.

Full disclosure: I don't like anything in my beer. I don't like fruity beer, I'm not a fan of seasonal or dark beer, and I certainly wasn't going to enjoy a spicy beer of any kind. Everyone fawns over IPAs and micro-breweries are springing up like Starbucks, but it's just not my thing.

Don't get me wrong, I'll tolerate those types of beer when out with friends, and I'll try just about anything once, but it's just not for me on a regular basis. Kind of like my relationship with vegetables: I know I must eat them, but I reserve the right to not enjoy them.

So, it was with much trepidation that I acquiesced for my friend's sake and gave pumpkin spice beer a try. It came in a tall, frosty mug rimmed with cinnamon sugar. I knew it would be a problem as it was being poured because it was much darker than the light, amber color I preferred. But my friend was so excited about it, and I knew she would be disappointed if I didn't like it. I resigned myself to make sure that I would put on a brave face no matter how disgusting it was. I'd channel my best El Exigente approval and give it a thumb's up. The last thing I needed was to spit it out like a scene from The Three Stooges.

But I loved it.

It was tasty, smooth, and most of all, the cinnamon sugar was fantastic. Previously, there wasn't anything with the word "pumpkin" in the title that I liked. To me, pumpkins had always been relegated to Halloween decorations and Thanksgiving dessert tables.

At the time, John Harvard's was the only brewery crafting a pumpkin spice beer. People would come from miles around to grab a growler and take it home. Soon, it became a tradition for me to procure the odd concoction every Thanksgiving.

Before you knew it, other local breweries were preparing a pumpkin spice variety, and soon, major breweries had picked up on the trend. Today, virtually every beer company offers a version of pumpkin spice beer, making it readily available.

Somehow, beer spiced with a flavor nobody seemed to care about started a trend. As companies scrambled to jump on the bandwagon, pumpkin spice suddenly began to creep into other products like a virus. Seemingly overnight, manufacturers began modifying their products with a pumpkin spice variety: coffee, tea, potato chips, gum,

ENOUGH ALREADY WITH PUMPKIN SPICE | 169

yogurt, cookies, milk, candy corn, pasta, vitamins, applesauce, cereal, and peanut butter.

I'd like to know who was clamoring for infusing pumpkin spice into these products? Has the market stalled to the point that the public is demanding a pumpkin spice Oreo cookie? Are people no longer eating Cheerios in October unless they are flavored with pumpkin spice? Did the Boy Scouts plead with Kraft to create a pumpkin spice marshmallow for s'mores? When will this insanity end?

There could be light at the end of the pumpkin spice tunnel, my friends. Once again, manufacturers oversaturated the market while trying to capitalize on a hot trend. Apparently, as the demand for pumpkin spice products starts to wane, companies are scrambling for a new fall flavor.

This September, Starbucks unveiled a new flavored latté, maple pecan. Our friends from the north know all too well the power of maple flavoring. Combine it with pecans, and how long before it infiltrates M&M's and Chobani Yogurt, creating a Game of Thrones-type situation on store shelves? Will you align with "House Pumpkin" or "House Maple Pecan?"

Sadly, John Harvard's closed its doors for good earlier this year. Although I can now get pumpkin spiced beer from virtually anywhere, I'm going to miss the anticipation and excitement in knowing the day was approaching when pumpkin spiced beer would be available.

Sorry, gotta go now. My pumpkin spice Pop-Tarts are ready.

A SANDY STORY

2017

As we approached the fifth anniversary of Superstorm Sandy here in the Northeast, I decided to tell this story.

The devastating hurricane that hit in late October of 2012 sent most Long Islanders into the dark ages for weeks and months. Some never recovered.

My family was spared the total devastation that others living closer to the water were unable to escape. I couldn't say the same for our friends Sheila and Dean, who lived right on the water on the South Shore of Massapequa.

Like other South Shore residents, they decided to stay in their home while the storm was raging around them. Soon, with the waters rising and surrounding their home, it was too late to evacuate. They were trapped.

This is the true, harrowing tale of their fight for survival as they attempted to escape their crumbling home with Mother Nature in full force around them.

Due to word-limit constraints, this column appeared in two-parts in the <u>Massapequa Observer</u>. I've condensed it into a single story for this collection.

A Sandy Story
By Paul DiSclafani

It's been five years since Long Island was ravaged by SuperStorm Sandy. Although we've been hit by our share of hurricanes and blizzards in the past, very few storms have been assigned the moniker of "catastrophic."

Many areas are prone to losing power during storms—after all, we do live on an island—but if the power is out for days, that would be unusual. Sandy changed all of that.

Numerous communities were devastated by the storm surge. Although people were inclined to rebuild, there was a lot of trepidation this time around. For most, rebuilding was their only option. Not many people had the option of letting their home go and moving somewhere else. And although New York State promised to help everyone rebuild, many have still not gotten a dime.

If you didn't experience it personally, you've undoubtedly heard or read stories about people who were without power for weeks. Families lost everything, including priceless memories, as the waters breached their foundations and washed it all away. There were numerous heartbreaking tales and images of people dragging furniture and possessions to the curb in the aftermath of the storm, now facing the unthinkable rebuilding process. We've seen this happen in other places and around the world, but here on Long Island? Where do you even start?

With the storm raging that night and no power inside, I ventured out to my car to listen to the radio and try to make sense of what was happening. We live just north of the LIRR tracks in Massapequa, so flooding was not a concern. We certainly had our share of wind damage and downed trees, losing fences and carports that flew into neighbor's yards like cheap umbrellas. But we had no idea what was going on just a mile or so away, where the shoreline could no longer hold back the water.

Our friends, Sheila and Dean, had moved to Massapequa earlier in the year. They settled into a beautiful little house at the end of East

Shore Drive, just south of Peninsula golf course. With a second-floor bedroom that overlooked the bay and the sunrise every morning, the house was perfect for the newly engaged couple. Both had grown children and were to be married that November, right after Thanksgiving. My wife met Sheila while waking our Labrador, Louie. Together with their lab, Jake, they developed a human and canine friendship that still exists today.

We all heard the dire warnings as the storm was making landfall up the Florida coast, which resulted in all of us running out for milk and bread. There was now an excellent chance of Long Island getting smacked, but it's just a storm, right? Batten down the hatches, pick up some batteries, and plan to work from home tomorrow.

During the afternoon, the news reports became more and more alarming. The rain and wind were intensifying, but when we heard the south shore of Nassau and Suffolk County were starting to evacuate, this started to get real. We offered our home as shelter for our friends who lived on the water, but like most Long Islanders, they were going to ride it out. They assured us that if things got bad, they were out of there.

While the storm raged outside their home, the water level increased about a foot over the bulkhead. Now the water was beginning to enter the house through Jake's doggie door in the washroom. Still, nothing to panic about, but there was going to be a colossal cleanup tomorrow, no doubt. They were expecting some flooding, and, quite frankly, there wasn't much they could do about it.

They headed upstairs to their bedroom and were watching *The Godfather* when the wind really began to howl. Looking out the huge picture window, they could only marvel at the power of mother nature, wishing they were seeing it on the National Geographic channel. In place of the bay's usual calm down at Unqua Point, they observed waves pushing the water into the canal and into their yard, lapping up against their back door.

That's when they noticed their neighbor's 25-foot boat being blown off its mooring.

Although their next-door neighbors fled before the storm hit, the wind was shaking the 25-foot boat they left behind. It was now sitting unsecured on a lift out of the water. The boat struggled against the roaring winds but was no match for Sandy's intensity, which achieved cyclone status and was now packing hurricane-force winds.

The unsecured boat was tossed like a toy off the lift. Watching in horror as it rode the rising tide closer and closer to the house, the boat finally nestled against the glass patio doors. But the whipping wind was manufacturing waves on the normally calm bay, forcing the boat through Sheila and Dean's fragile patio doors like a bull in a China shop, taking out the kitchen wall directly below them.

With the structure brutally damaged, they fled down the stairs as the savagery of the storm took up residence inside their exposed living room, like an unwanted house guest. There was more than a foot of water inside now and it was rising rapidly with no barrier between the raging bay waters and their living room.

Grabbing Jake and heading out the front door, they were engulfed by cold, chest-deep water flowing through the street like river rapids. Frightened and unsure what to do next, they attempted to traverse the furious current, only to find that Jake was having no part of it, and heading back to the house. Snatching the terrified dog, they fought against rushing water, forcing their way across the street to a neighbor's house, only to find no one home. The wind was roaring, the rain was relentless, and there was no turning back.

Exhausted from the physical and mental anguish, they trekked to another house, hoping to seek shelter. Pounding on the stranger's door, they hoped someone would respond and take pity on them. When the startled strangers answered the door and reluctantly let them in, the water inside their house was already past the two-foot mark.

Outside, the unrelenting wind continued to push the water down the street as East Shore Road ceased to exist. Now, only water covered the distance between the houses on opposite sides of the street. There was an eerie hum as the wind droned on, drowning out the silence of this awful night. There was no power, no communications, and apparently, no escape. Perched atop the living room couches, what little hope they clung to was starting to wane as the water began to lap at their feet.

When day broke, the sun came out, and the wind was gone, but East Shore Road had vanished. Still wet and cold, Sheila and Dean waded across the newly formed river to survey the damage to their home, but it was a total loss. A boat was wedged halfway into their kitchen and was holding up the rest of the house. Carefully, they collected a few things and headed north, targeting Merrick Road and higher ground.

Slogging through the murky water like refugees in a zombie-like trance, they observed onlookers stopping to take pictures of the devastation. But no one offered to help the wet strangers and their dog as they continued their quest for dry land.

Sometime after 11:00 a.m., the weary travelers arrived at our door, exhausted and forlorn. Although we had no power, we certainly had a working shower, plenty of food, and dry clothes to offer them. Unable to communicate with them over these grueling hours, just seeing them safe was a relief.

Eventually, they rebuilt their house on East Shore Road but never returned. They wouldn't chance a possible repeat of the pain and horror they endured. The wedding still took place right after Thanksgiving. Eventually, Sheila and Dean settled into a new house in Massapequa Park, way north of the LIRR tracks and the soggy memory of East Shore Road..

With the recent spate of hurricanes that have battered island coastlines, we worry that one of them will be heading our way again. Many have generators now to keep the electricity running. Folks down on the water have been raising their houses off the ground to avoid flooding.

Nobody wants to go through that again, but it's not up to us, is it?

MY APPLIANCES ARE PLOTTING AGAINST ME

2018

Owning a home means you have appliances available to keep things running smoothly. As a homeowner, you are responsible for maintaining (or replacing) those appliances as the years move on. Renting a home means someone else is responsible for those appliances running smoothly.

We ran into a rough stretch where everything seemed to be breaking down at once. Sitting back and thinking about it, I wondered if it was some sort of organized slow down by the union our appliances were part of.

Many moons ago, I was a union representative for Local 1199, so I know how powerful a union can be. I decided that since I am now part of Management, I might look at things differently.

I know it's silly, but why not have fun with the thought?

My Appliances are Plotting Against Me
By Paul DiSclafani

Don't look now, but I believe my household appliances organized a coordinated work slow down, which could lead to a full-blown work stoppage. Although I haven't been presented with a complete list of demands yet, there is definitely something fishy going on.

I think I run a reasonably progressive union shop without overworking my appliances. I recently hired a Roomba to assist our vacuum with the daily grind of picking up after the always-shedding Louie the Labrador. Without threatening the seniority of our trusty Kenmore, the Roomba is more of an assistant. Plus, the Roomba gets weekends off.

When we realized that the freezer's size on our new side-by-side fridge wasn't cutting it, we hired a separate freezer unit to take the pressure off. Some of my appliances have to work occasional overtime, like the TV and central air conditioning. Still, they are maintained and kept in good running condition following the manufacturers' recommendations.

Last year, our washer went out on disability for a few weeks while waiting for new parts to arrive. The thought never occurred to us to have it replaced; and since it got back from rehab, so far, so good.

In my house, the appliances seem to revolt in groups. A few years ago, both the microwave and refrigerator needed to be replaced within days of each other. Before that, both the washer and dryer went out simultaneously, like they were in cahoots with each other. Although we've had a few years of labor peace, it seems the machines are getting restless again.

It started a few months ago when the coffee machine unexpectedly retired along with my alarm clock. Then in a single week, the air conditioning, fridge, and dishwasher all began leaking water. What are the odds of that?

I understand that things break down. At my age, I experience that every morning when I get out of bed. An ache here, a crack there, I get it. Things get old and break down. But I never thought that appliances calculated birthdays in dog years.

Can't these appliances coordinate their breakdowns? Everyone can't go on vacation at the same time, which leads to chaos. Wouldn't it be great if the shift supervisor for the dishwasher worked together with the fridge, so they didn't both need to be repaired at the same time?

Although we negotiated a new collective bargaining agreement with both the fridge and air conditioning unions (for now), the dishwasher had enough and just quit on us. Now I needed to search for a new dishwasher.

We weren't looking for anything fancy, just a basic replacement. We went to the PC Richards' Employment Agency and were presented with several job candidates. When inquiring about the differences between the $500 and $1,200 models, we were told the more expensive models had more features. For more money, you could have multiple wash cycles, control it with your smartphone, and it operates more quietly.

Why would you need any wash cycle other than "clean the dishes"? I don't know about you, but since my dishwasher isn't in the living room or the bedroom, I like to be able to hear it, so I know I turned it on. And to be honest, do I need anything else in my life that I can control with my smartphone? Tell you what, when a $1,200 dishwasher can clear the dishes from the table and put them back in the cabinets, I'll consider it.

Luckily, the $500 dishwasher accepted the job offer, along with an excellent benefits package, including extended medical coverage. We are looking forward to a long-lasting relationship with it starting next Thursday. Until then, we're stocking up on paper plates and plastic cutlery.

What, you thought we were going to hire a scab to do the dishes until then? I told you this was a union shop...

MY MOTHER'S BEST HALLOWEEN

2018

It's hard to imagine your parents having a life before you came along. They dated, had crazy friends, and probably did crazy things.

One memorable Halloween night when I was still in high school, my mother's friends from work showed up at my house after dinner. They coerced my usually unspontaneous mother into joining them for an adventure.

I remembered that night quite vividly but didn't understand what it meant to my mother until much later in life.

My Mother's Best Halloween
By Paul DiSclafani

My mother was part of the generation you saw depicted on TV sitcoms like *I Love Lucy, Leave it to Beaver,* or *The Honeymooners.* Wives of that era didn't work for a living. They might have before they got married, but once they started a family, their job was raising the children and running the household. Suddenly, there was a mortgage to consider and household bills to pay. Many were forced to rejoin the workforce once the kids were in school. My mother was no different.

Except, having a job didn't relieve them of their responsibilities at home. They still took care of the house, cooked all the meals, and made sure you did your homework. But for those few hours out of the house every afternoon, they could escape. They had friends you didn't know, went out to restaurants for lunch, and had a real social life.

The mother I know was not prone to spontaneous acts of youthful exuberance—at least not when I was in high school. I'm sure my parents did lots of wild and crazy things before I came along; it's just that I've never seen it. They've always been Mom and Dad. Old black-and-white photos of them as young adults with relatives and friends told a partial story as everyone was always smiling and laughing. But I never saw her do anything remotely spontaneous that was just, well, let's call it, silly.

Except for this one time.

We had finished dinner one Halloween when the doorbell rang. Back then, it wasn't unusual for a few stragglers looking for candy to venture out after dark. I answered the door and was expecting teenagers covered in shaving cream. Instead, I was shocked to find two of my mother's co-workers, Gracie and Lee, dressed up like bums. They were wearing old clothes, carrying shopping bags, yelling "Trick or Treat!"

Everyone had a good laugh when suddenly strange noises were coming from the back porch. As my mother opened the back door, two more of her friends lunged out, scaring the bejeebers out of her. I never saw her laugh so hard! Right before our eyes, a group of 40-something women was transforming into teenagers, and my mother was right in the middle of it.

Gracie, the ringleader, convinced my mother to go with them as they headed to my Aunt Jean's house (just a few blocks away) to scare her. Without hesitation, she changed into some old clothes to join them on this crazy adventure. Imagine my mother going on an adventure!

My brother and I were stunned at this turn of events. Could this be our mother? She just didn't do these types of things—whose mother did?

They succeeded in their mission to scare Aunt Jean and somehow convinced her to join the crazy train. They squeezed into Gracie's car and headed to, of all places, Pinelawn Cemetery, walking amongst the dead and laughing like teenagers.

Soon, our regular mother was returned to us undamaged. She went back to enjoying life and her family. She slipped back into her familiar role like a comfortable pair of shoes.

As we were reminiscing about their adventure the other day with my Aunt Jean, their eyes brightened, and their smiles broadened. The sisters remembered that long-forgotten Halloween night like yesterday, recalling the craziness and bringing back a flood of memories. It was one of the best nights my mother could remember. It was undoubtedly her most memorable Halloween.

At the time, my brother and I could not believe what we were seeing. This was so out of character for my mother; I think we were just stunned as the events of the evening unfolded. But my father seemed to take this unusual occurrence in stride.

Then again, maybe he had already witnessed this side of our mother and was secretly glad to see it reappear. After all, our parents were young kids at some point, often doing fun, spontaneous things.

It was nice to get a glimpse of that life and see our parents differently, even if it was for only one night.

TRYING THE IMPOSSIBLE WHOPPER

2019

This was not only a fun column to write, it was also a fun experience. I like to give my readers an inside look into my life, including stupid things like this.

Since I consider myself a newspaper reporter with his own column, I went out to report on a story that was intriguing to me. After being bombarded by commercials for Burger King's new "Impossible Whopper," I finally decided to give it a try.

I no longer eat a lot of fast food, but "The King" has always been my place of choice. I decided to give it a try, and the results ended up in this column.

Trying the Impossible Whopper
By Paul DiSclafani

Unless you have been living under a rock, you've seen the commercials for Burger King's new "Impossible Whopper." Happy customers, with puzzled looks on their faces, were trying it for the first time. Most couldn't believe what they were eating was not a regular Whopper.

Of course, I'm sure we will never see the outtakes of people spitting onto the ground or trashing the new product in any way. Still, I was curious, and inquiring minds wanted to know.

A few months ago, in this column, I picked the Whopper as my last meal of choice in the unlikely event that I end up on Death Row. Therefore, I consider myself an aficionado of Burger King and the Whopper.

After taking my mother to a doctor's appointment, she wanted to treat me to lunch, so we stopped at Burger King. When we pulled into the parking lot in Seaford, I noticed the signs for the Impossible Whopper announcing it as a "limited time only" promotion. It was now or never, so I thought, why not?

Cautiously, I asked the counter person what would happen if I didn't like the Impossible Whopper? Since the price was a dollar more than a regular Whopper, I wondered if there would be some sort of a money-back guarantee. Apparently not.

"You'll like it," she enthusiastically told me, "Everyone loves it."

Yeah, and the Titanic was unsinkable...

Looking at the pictures on the menu board, it looked exactly like the regular Whopper. Instead of the traditional white and yellow wrapper, the Impossible Whopper came wrapped in eco-green colored paper. After unwrapping it, I opened the bun to inspect the patty, something I've never done with a Whopper before.

It looked like a burger patty, even having the same texture. I've cooked veggie burgers on the grill alongside regular hamburgers, and there is no comparison. The look, feel, and taste are completely different. But this was no ordinary veggie burger. I reassembled the Impossible Whopper, closed my eyes, and took a bite.

To be honest, this was impossible.

If I didn't know better, I might have had a hard time telling the difference. The more bites I took, the more I realized that many different flavors were attacking my taste buds. The actual taste of the patty itself was just a tiny part of the equation. It was flame-broiled and smothered in ketchup and mayo, supplemented with onions, lettuce, tomatoes, and pickles. It certainly didn't NOT taste like a regular Whopper.

After finishing the Impossible Whopper, I decided that if it were indeed healthier than a regular Whopper (which checks in at about 1,200 calories), maybe I would consider it every now and then. It certainly sounds healthier. It's made from plants' roots and is infused with coconut and sunflower oil, allowing it to sizzle when cooked. Maybe we can save a few cows along the way?

But upon further review, it's not. It's got about the same nutritional value as a regular Whopper. You only save about 30 calories, and everything else that's bad for you—sodium, trans fat, etc., is about the same. On top of that, it will cost you a dollar more.

If it's not healthier (and more expensive to boot), then what's the point? I guess if there's a market for decaffeinated coffee and non-alcoholic beer, why not a Whopper that tastes like beef but doesn't have any meat?

I'm not sure I'm ready for something that isn't what I think it is. Let's be honest, you're not really making a healthy choice when you choose a Whopper, yet we order them anyway. Nobody goes out of their way for a Burger King salad. With that said, is there really any reason to order an Impossible Whopper when the regular Whopper is still available.

Thanks, but no thanks.

With apologies to Elsie the Cow, whether it's my last meal or not, I'll take my Whopper with beef.

WHY YOU SHOULD RESPECT THE FLAG

2017

I wrote this column in honor of Veterans Day in 2017. It came at the height of NFL athletes choosing to kneel during the National Anthem to protest social injustices.

Generally, I try to avoid political topics for obvious reasons. And although this seemed to be more politically motivated than socially motivated, I wanted to address it but look at it a little differently.

We were having a discussion at my brother's house one evening, addressing the athletes who have chosen to kneel while the National Anthem was playing. As a Boy Scout leader for years (both of my nephews made Eagle Scout), my brother said he was preparing the annual flag etiquette presentation for the Boy Scouts. He proceeded to share some of what was in the presentation.

Quite frankly, it was interesting and inspiring at the same time.

I was so moved by his passion for the topic, I did some additional research about our National Anthem's origins and penned this column.

Why You Should Respect the Flag
By Paul DiSclafani

Before you start reading, understand this is not a political column. Everyone has an opinion on professional athletes choosing to use our National Anthem's playing as a forum to protest social injustices.

Of course, every American has the right to protest what they want, when they want, in whatever form they choose. Even the Supreme Court of the United States has ruled disrespecting the flag is no longer punishable by law. People are within their rights to disrespect the flag or choose the playing of our National Anthem as the time and place to protest, but that doesn't make it right.

My generation was taught the basics of flag etiquette at a very young age. We learned that our military fought and died for that flag. But those brave men and women didn't make the ultimate sacrifice for a piece of cloth. They made that sacrifice for what it represents.

My brother Tony has been involved with the Boy Scouts since my nephews were little, and both achieved the highest honor, Eagle Scout. Still involved in scouting, Tony prepares the annual presentation about flag etiquette. He spoke about what the flag represents.

"The flag is thought of as a trooper, a comrade, a soldier," he told me. "It's to be honored and respected. It's a living thing that should always be properly displayed and cared for. In battle, no one is ever left behind. You certainly wouldn't leave your flag behind to be captured by the enemy. You don't let it touch the ground, you don't sit on it, and there is a right and wrong way when displaying it. When it becomes tattered and no longer fitting for display, it should be destroyed in a dignified, honored fashion."

Did you know the flag is considered an officer in the military, hence saluted every morning? It should be hoisted briskly and lowered ceremoniously. It represents a living country and therefore is regarded as a living thing. When displaying a flag pin on your clothing, it is always displayed on the left side, just over your heart.

The flag is presented to the surviving family of anyone who has served in the military. Still, it's not just handed to the widow. It is slowly and carefully folded into a triangle, honoring the soldiers' tri-cornered hats during the Revolutionary War. When folded, the red and white stripes are wrapped in blue to symbolize nightfall.

He reminded me the flag itself is not what you are fighting for. It's what the flag represents.

"If you were trapped in a foxhole, you might take one last look at a picture of your wife and kids before you went out to continue the fight," he said. "You are not fighting for that picture; you're fighting for what that picture represents."

The flag symbolizes to the rest of the world what the United States represents: the field of blue for honor, white for purity, and red for the blood we shed. World War II veterans overseas often described seeing our flag flying at a compound, knowing they were at home. It gave them sanctuary; it gave them peace.

This past June 14, we celebrated the 240th anniversary of adopting the stars and stripes as a symbol of our nation. We may be of diverse backgrounds, races, or religions, but we come together for one common good, our country.

In 1814, Francis Scott Key penned "The Star-Spangled Banner," which was adopted as The National Anthem more than 100 years later. As a lawyer during the War of 1812, he rowed into the Baltimore harbor, advancing on the British warship Minden. Traveling with only a truce flag and a letter from President James Madison, Key brokered the release of a prisoner on the ship, his friend Dr. Beanes. However, the men were detained on board as the boat was preparing to attack Fort McHenry.

During the bombardment, Key observed the stars and stripes flying over the fort until darkness fell. He could only see the fort returning fire back at the British, proving that they had not surrendered. When daylight returned, so did the flag, motivating him to jot down the inspiring opening words:

> ***O say, can you see by the dawn's early light***
> ***What so proudly we hailed at the twilight's last gleaming***
> ***Whose broad stripes and bright stars***

> ***Through the perilous fight***
> ***O'er the ramparts we watched***
> ***Were so gallantly streaming?***

So, the next time you're at a ballgame, or any event where you are asked to rise from your seat, remove your hat, and join in the singing of The National Anthem, make the right choice for the right reason.

And when you encounter a veteran this weekend (or anytime), shake their hand and thank them for their service.

WHAT HAPPENED TO TRICK OR TREATING?

2019

My generation's parents are much more protective of their kids (for better or worse) than our parents were for us. Sometimes it's more than justified as the world around us has changed into a scary, more dangerous place.

Unfortunately, I think that has taken all the fun out of the fine art of Trick or Treating on Halloween. It seems each year, we have been getting fewer and fewer kids ringing our doorbell to request candy in exchange for avoiding tricks.

I was trying to explore what phenomenon has led us down this path. Still, I couldn't help reminiscing about what Halloween used to be like.

What Happened to Trick or Treating?
By Paul DiSclafani

From my childhood through becoming an adult, Halloween on our Massapequa block was always swarming with kids trick-or-treating. We needed multiple bags of candy or other pre-packaged treats to satisfy the hordes of goblins, bums, superheroes, sports figures, cartoon characters, and princesses.

Barring rainy weather, which for some reason doesn't seem to happen too often on Halloween, our bell was ringing all day and night. During the day, kids adorned in their costumes happily yelled the required phrase "trick or treat," holding open their bags or baskets to score some treats.

When we were kids, our parents let us go from door to door by ourselves until it got dark. We had a simple rule—be back before the streetlights came on. Of course, once the night took over, so did the not-so-young kids. Some were still dressing up, but it mainly was a half-hearted attempt as something simple, like a pirate, zombie, or football player.

Instead of declaring "trick-or-treat," they just rang the bell and waited for you to drop something into their makeshift goody bag, usually an old pillowcase. A few didn't even bother dressing up, while others were covered from head-to-toe with shaving cream. Either way, you always needed to have candy available for them, or you might end up on the wrong side of a trick-or-treat.

Sometime in the early '80s, paranoia began gripping the suburbs with reports of adults tampering with candy and putting razor blades in apples. That changed everything. My kids were always allowed to keep all their loot, but only after we inspected each and every piece. Part of our Halloween tradition was sitting at the dining room table and performing a complete examination of everything in that bag. Anything not wrapped was automatically tossed, while wrapped candy was checked to make sure the wrapper wasn't tampered with in any way.

I think the art of neighborhood trick-or-treating is dying a slow death. In the last few years, we've had very few vampires or Pokémon ring our bell, even when Halloween fell on a Saturday. I've had to reluctantly eat my share of leftover Halloween candies and treats.

Well, somebody's gotta take one for the team, right?

Some schools are now hosting Halloween walk-throughs, where the kids stroll the corridors, stopping at each classroom to get candy. Our local shopping area in Massapequa Park can be a gold mine for kids as they go from store-to-store accumulating loot. It's a great haul for the kids, except when they stop by the local dental office. They usually end up with a toothbrush instead of candy.

But that type of trick-or-treating is so antiseptic. The kids are herded like cattle from store to store, robotically holding their bags open with no regard for what is being dropped into them. Kids needed to pay attention to their goodies in my day. Sometimes you would run into friends, and the first thing you would ask is, "What are the Snyder's giving out?" If you found a house paying off with cool candy, you tried to sneak back a second time. Setting up an assembly line where kids just show up and get candy without working for it is undoubtedly safer, but in reality is it any fun for the kids?

It's sad to think what the kids of today are missing out on. They'll never know the thrill of knocking on a stranger's door and risking abduction for candy that your parents could have purchased for you. Meanwhile, even an eyewitness would have trouble identifying a kid being snatched. You know how many Batman's there were out there?

I genuinely miss the old Halloween when kids worked the neighborhood dressed in costumes, ringing doorbells, and daring you with a hearty "trick or treat."

Then again, the fewer kids that show up at my house, the more loot for me.

CELEBRATING THANKSGIVING ITALIAN STYLE

2018

Growing up, we had no greater holiday than Thanksgiving at my grandmother's house in Brooklyn.

When gathering with family in more recent years, we constantly reflected on those carefree days filled with way too much food and way too much fun and memories. Both sets of my grandparents had seven children, so it never mattered which one we were attending. It was always organized chaos.

I decided to open the door to my grandmother's basement and let my readers inside to see, hear, and smell what went on during an Italian Thanksgiving.

Mangia!

Celebrating Thanksgiving Italian Style
By Paul DiSclafani

There is nothing like Thanksgiving to kick off your holiday season. While December is filled with numerous multi-cultural and religious observances, Thanksgiving is a truly national holiday celebrated by all people, regardless of race, religion, or political affiliation. It's a gathering of family and friends to share a meal and reflect on things they are thankful for. It becomes an eating challenge for Italian families that even the stars of *Man vs. Food* would struggle with.

Once the big day arrives, grandma's tranquil basement kitchen resembles a subway station at rush hour, overflowing with people scurrying in all directions. With Jimmy Roselli crooning in the background, aunts of all shapes, sizes, and hairdos were busy preparing different dishes. My uncles were safely upstairs, claiming every available couch and "relaxing" (which I thought was another word for snoring). While tomato sauce simmered on the gas burners, a giant turkey browned in the oven. Every now and then, one of our aunts would summon us to view the enormous bird as they pulled it out for basting, ensuring a moist, beautiful tan. Only the older cousins were allowed a chance at sucking up the bubbling juice with the turkey baster, releasing it slowly over the beast.

If you think you have overeaten at a family Thanksgiving, you ain't seen nothing like an Italian Thanksgiving at my Grandmother's house. Ever have a Thanksgiving meal that started with lasagna? We did, all the time. The food just came in waves, like a tsunami.

Sometimes we started with antipasto or soup, leading into lasagna. After a short commercial break, my father would begin carving the turkey, which was bigger than some of my cousins. As the silverware sat nervously upon neatly folded napkins, the table began to fill with vegetables, stuffing, mashed potatoes, gravy, hot rolls, and butter.

Soon, there was food flying everywhere. Women were hustling to fill the plates of both the kids and the men. They took care of everyone before sitting down and enjoying the meal they spent hours preparing. And to think, just 20 minutes ago, we were stuffing our faces with lasagna.

Some requested white meat, others dark, but we would always reserve one of the giant turkey legs for the traditional family photo. There always seemed to be an infant grandchild on my grandfather's lap, holding that colossal turkey leg in their tiny little hands, like Bam-Bam from *The Flintstones*. Our albums are filled with those photos. It's a family tradition that we still follow today with our children.

As the carnage surrounding the turkey dinner waned, the men

retreated upstairs to "relax" again. At the same time, the women performed the task of cleaning up and resetting the table for dessert. In the blink of an eye, the turkey was gone, and all the side dishes disappeared. Magically, a mountain of Italian pastries and traditional baked pies appeared. Coffee and demitasse pots were chugging away as the crowd began to gather once again. Soon, we kids would be wolfing down pie or ice cream topped with chocolate syrup. Meanwhile, the adults settled for cannoli and other artery-clogging treats.

And just when everyone had caught their breath to relax and watch some TV, someone would break out the leftover turkey and rolls to make sandwiches.

As you got older, you were able to survey the room and truly understand where you came from. You didn't need a DNA test from 23-and-Me, or an ancestry history to confirm you were a part of this family. My mother and father had six brothers and sisters each, so there were plenty of aunts, uncles, and cousins to go around. Everywhere you looked, you saw a part of you in everyone. You had your grandfather's hairline, your aunt's eyebrows, and your uncle's waistline. You were blessed with your mother's sense of humor and your father's eyes. And when you look at your children, you see a part of everyone in them, also.

This is your family, for better or worse. They defined you and helped lead you on the path to who you are today.

And they always made sure you had a turkey sandwich to go home with.

REMEMBERING JOHN LENNON

2018

In January of 2009, the Rock and Roll Hall of Fame opened an annex in New York City, SoHo to be exact. Inside, artifacts focused on New York area legends like Simon and Garfunkel, Billy Joel, Bruce Springsteen, and the Punk Rock movement.

The featured exhibit was dedicated to John Lennon, the New York Years.

I visited twice, once with friends and again with my wife and son Kevin. Kevin was blossoming into an accomplished drummer, and I wanted him to see some of rock and roll history first hand.

Unlike my first visit, I felt more like a tour guide for Kevin, pointing out some great artists and regaling him with stories of wild concerts I had attended. I looked forward to seeing the John Lennon exhibit with him and hoped he would appreciate Lennon's genius as one of the world's greatest musicians.

As we walked into the exhibit, which was put together by Yoko Ono, I began pointing things out to him. We stood silently for a few moments before the display of John's iconic eyeglasses. Positioned as if they were casually left on an end table, one of the lenses was covered in blood in stark contrast to the backdrop, a blurry shot of the New York City skyline. I was so overcome with emotion, I couldn't speak. I sat down in front of several video screens that showed images of John's life in New York and found myself crying. At least I wasn't alone. Many other people were letting their feelings out in the same way.

When the anniversary of his death came around in 2018, I decided to write a tribute column to John, recalling that night in 1980 when I learned of his death from, of all people, Howard Cosell on <u>Monday Night Football</u>.

Remembering John Lennon
By Paul DiSclafani

My generation will probably never get over the Beatles' breakup in 1970. Still, as the decade came to an end, at least we came to grips that they were never getting back together. While some of them contributed to each other's solo albums, the rift was way too deep for a complete reunion.

Although the individual Beatles continued to make music after the breakup, John Lennon chose to go on hiatus after his son Sean's birth in 1975, becoming a full-time father. After initially creating a mild furor with his decision to no longer perform or produce commercially released music, fans would not deny him his privacy and respected his decision. We still had plenty of John Lennon music to listen to.

During the summer of 1980, word began to seep out that Lennon and Yoko Ono were in a recording studio. Before you knew it, *Double Fantasy* was being released in October, restoring balance to the World again. A combination of six tracks each from John and Yoko initially disappointed Beatles fans who were hoping for an entire Lennon album, but you take what you can get, right?

The Lennon songs were wonderfully written and beautiful to listen to. He touched our hearts with "Beautiful Boy (Darling Boy)," "Just Like Starting Over," and "Woman." He even answered the question as to what he had been doing for the last five years. "Watching the Wheels" explained that he was just tired and exhausted from being a Beatle and just needed to let it go. We all sympathized with him as we were growing older together. Many of us were just getting started in adult life and were ready for Lennon to take us along with him to the next step through his music. After all, he and the Beatles helped shape our lives.

And just like that, less than two months later, it was over.

As I sat alone in my living room on December 8, 1980, watching the end of the Monday Night Football game, Howard Cosell broke the news to an unsuspecting national audience in his famous staccato delivery.

> *"An unspeakable tragedy confirmed to us by ABC News. John Lennon, outside of his apartment on the west side of New York City, the most famous, perhaps, of all the Beatles, shot twice in the back, rushed to Roosevelt Hospital. Dead. On. Arrival."*

What did he say?

I watched the Patriots kicker trot out onto the field to attempt a game-winning field goal, but I thought I heard Howard say something about John Lennon. As I moved closer to the TV to hear better, I heard them talking about it. No doubt, John Lennon was gone.

There was no internet to confirm the horror. No Facebook, Instagram, or Twitter. There were no social media platforms in which to share your grief, just the telephone. So, I called my friend Bruce to ask him if he was watching the game, breaking the "never call after 9:00 p.m." rule. My memories of the events from that evening are blurry, but we both shared the magnitude of the tragedy together, with tears and disbelief.

As a budding adult, I got my first real dose of reality—life was not fair. Here was a revered musician who never harmed a soul and only made the world a better place, gunned down in his prime for no good reason. The evening Mark Chapman decided to fire those shots, Lennon was returning from a recording session. He decided to stop for a fan who wanted an autograph, just like he had probably done thousands of times. In shock and sadness, we felt the peace and love of the '60s and '70s were now gone.

But they say time heals all wounds, and while we are still saddened by Lennon's untimely death, we can focus on his legacy of music and how he lived. I think he would have imagined it that way.

A LOVE AFFAIR WITH MY SNOWBLOWER

2017

My home has a beautifully paved circular driveway. One side is a single driveway, while the other is a double-wide driveway. In the middle is an arch. In layman's terms, that's the equivalent of four standard driveways. I can comfortably park more than six vehicles.

Next door, where my mother lives, is a long driveway that extends from the street all the way to the back of the house. We can easily get four cars in that driveway.

I tell you all of this because I want you to know what a pain in the you-know-what it is to take care of all that automobile real estate when it snows.

At first, I thought my snowblower was man's greatest invention. But I found myself cursing it when the snow was too deep or too heavy. Finally, after replacing my snowblower twice, I went out and purchased an Ariens, the Cadillac of snow removal equipment.

A Love Affair With My Snowblower
By Paul DiSclafani

It started out innocently with a forecast of 1 to 3 inches, quickly morphing into 3 to 6 inches of snow overnight Friday into Saturday.

Although we experienced temperatures close to 60 on Tuesday, here we were just three days later, facing an approaching snowstorm.

Like many Long Island homeowners, we spent that Friday evening preparing—inventorying rock salt quantities and positioning the shovels just outside the front doors. We extricated the boots, hats, and gloves from their summer home under the stairs and accounted for all our scarves. Like they have been saying for the last few years on *Game of Thrones*, Winter is coming. Whether or not the weather guy got it right this time is irrelevant. Sooner or later, we are inevitably going to get snow here in the Northeast.

If you are a regular reader of this column, you know that my love/hate relationship with snow is almost all hate. My mother has adorable pictures of me as a child, standing on gigantic snow piles, wrapped up like that kid from *A Christmas Story* with only my eyes visible. I recall enjoying sleigh riding and making snowmen as much as the next kid. However, my vivid memories of the events are the constricting preparation to get outside and the inevitable wetness accompanying the meltdown once back inside. But who doesn't love a snow day at that age?

As I grew older, snow days meant more than just a day off from school. You were no longer building a snowman and watching as your father and uncles shoveled the driveway and sidewalks of everyone within walking distance. Now, you were a participant. You most likely had your own car to shovel out. Suddenly, those romantic images of a winter wonderland turned into a nightmare every time the Town of Oyster Bay snow plow came barreling down your block after you just cleared the driveway.

Things changed dramatically when you got married and owned a home. Your father and uncles are now depending on you to help them. What happened to the neighborhood kids looking to make a couple of bucks? They were everywhere when I was in my twenties and couldn't afford them, but they have become extinct when I need them the most.

After years of struggling with shovels and backaches, I bought a snowblower. When I was a kid, every neighborhood had one or two guys with snowblowers, steering their noisy monsters up and down their driveways. We'd marvel at how high the snow would be expelled, arching over parked cars. They were so happy to be piloting the blower, they would do four or five of their neighbor's houses. Of course, my house was never in their geographic area.

I'll never forget the first time I fired up my snowblower and the feeling of power it gave me. No longer would I struggle with the back-breaking drudgery of snow removal. Modern machinery was doing the work for me. In my eyes, this was man's greatest achievement since the toaster. If I wasn't worried about my eyelids freezing shut, I would have been weeping with joy.

I've upgraded my snowblower a few times through the years, each time getting bigger and better. Wider mouth, better wheels, 2-stage thrower, electric start, even a headlight. Yes, I think I'm in love with my Ariens snowblower. As a Mets fan, I even love its bright orange color.

Was it expensive? You bet it was.

Was it worth it? Every penny.

The depth limitations of my early blowers required two or three passes during a massive storm. And if the snow was on the heavy side, fuhgeddaboudit. Now, I wait until the snow has stopped and just fire up the Ariens. Oh, the sweet sound of victory.

No snowblower is perfect, but this one is close. Maybe someday I'll turn into a snowbird and fly south for the winter, leaving behind the freezing weather and snow for the younger generation. Until then, my Ariens will get me through another winter.

After all, the South has those hideous Palmetto bugs...

YOU NEVER STOP BEING A PARENT, EVER

2017

If you have children, regardless of their ages, you know what becoming a parent is all about. You don't stop worrying about them just because they are grown and on their own.

I never understood why, as a married adult, my mother still wanted me to call her when we arrived at our vacation destination. But as my kids got older, I started to understand.

Having children might be an 18-year commitment legally, but, in actuality, the commitment lasts a lifetime.

This column helped me garner Third Place in the 2018 Press Club of Long Island Media Awards in the "Narrative-Column" category.

You Never Stop Being a Parent, Ever
By Paul DiSclafani

I'm 60 years old, and when I go on vacation with my wife, I still have to call my 85-year-old mother to let her know I got there. As a kid, this was a terrible nuisance. As a young adult, it was completely unnecessary. As a parent of adult children, I finally understand it.

My mother always told me it eased her mind knowing that I had arrived safely.

"You never stop being a parent," she said. "As long as my eyes are open, I'll worry about you and your brother."

I never thought much about it, but as my adult boys (28 and 25) get older, it seems that I do worry about them, even though I can no longer protect them like I did when they were little. In my eyes, they will always be 12 and 9.

Following my mother's lead, when they were kids, I required they call me when arriving at a friend's house for a play date, even if it was just down the block. If they changed location for any reason, I wanted to know. I needed to move my mental "pushpin" from one place on the imaginary map in my mind to another.

During their early years, parents provide their kids with the guidance, support, and protection they need, essentially making most of their decisions for them. You bought their clothes, you had the final say on what movies they saw, and you certainly had veto power on tattoos and piercings. You were the parent, after all.

Sure, they can pick the instrument they want to play or the activity they want to sign up for, but you will not let them quit school at 16 and join the circus, are you? You may not be able to steer them to the college or career you prefer, but you are certainly going to do your best to make sure they go to college or a trade school.

Young adults need to begin making decisions on their own at some point. You have invested almost half your life, instilling values into them and helping them grow, but it's time to let go. The only problem is, you just can't.

Unfortunately, you can only offer advice from the stands now; you are no longer the manager. You can shout things at them and hope they hear you, but they no longer have to listen to you. It's more frustrating as you both get older.

You'd think that with all this adult experience available, our children would take advantage of that knowledge, avoiding the pitfalls and mistakes they are eventually headed for. But that's not how it works. You can warn them 100 times not to touch the stove because it's hot, but they don't understand it until they find out for themselves.

When I was in my 20s, I never understood what my parents were trying to tell me since, of course, I knew better. It wasn't until later in life that I realized they were usually right. And now it's my turn to be the old man that yells at the clouds.

They will always be my kids, no matter how old we both get. I'll still try and protect them when I can and shake my head in frustration when I can't. The same way I smiled and wholly ignored my parents, I'm sure they smile and completely ignore me. At some point, they will see that I was right all along, but that's not going to happen until they can reach up and touch the stove for themselves. We can only hope that when they do, they don't get seriously burned.

Today, both my children love traveling, having already visited places my wife and I have only dreamed of going to. But it doesn't matter where they go or how they get there. I still want a text message when they arrive so I can move that pushpin...

THE MAGIC OF SANTA

2018

This is the last piece I've selected for this collection.

The Winter Holidays are near and dear to my heart because they are all about family.

In what has become standard operating procedure in early December, one of my kids asked me what I wanted for Christmas. It made me think about how I had been answering that question my entire life. My earliest memories of visiting a "store" Santa was the pressure of having an answer ready for when he asked me that question. Like the kid from <u>A Christmas Story</u>, I didn't want to blow it.

Santa has been an important part of our lives as kids and again when we had our own children. We, as parents, wanted to continue the magic of Santa for our kids into their teens and beyond. That's what this column was all about.

One thing you could always count on was the Magic of Santa. He never disappoints...

The Magic of Santa
By Paul DiSclafani

"What do you want for Christmas?"

We have been answering that question ever since the first time our parents placed us on the lap of a store Santa. I'm sure none of us remember what we asked for at that first encounter with St. Nick, but as you got older, your answer was very important.

Like me, you probably spent a few months trying to decide what to ask Santa for. You didn't want to waste it on something ridiculous, like a pony or a spaceship. You compared notes with your cousins and schoolmates. No, you had to think long and hard about it.

Back then, we believed in the magic of Santa, never questioning the logistics behind it. There was no need to. The North Pole, flying reindeer, visiting every house in one night; Santa's magic explained everything. With all that is going on in today's world, we need someone we can trust, and Santa rarely disappoints.

My fondest childhood memories were getting up early on Christmas morning to find out if Santa had come. Of course, we couldn't open any presents before daylight, but that didn't mean we couldn't look at what was there, right? We had to be like ninjas, even though we didn't know what a ninja was back then. We had to slowly sneak by our parent's bedroom to get into the living room, where the Christmas tree was.

There were plenty of presents from Mom and Dad, but we were specifically looking for the gifts we asked Santa for. Sometimes we might have to shake the box or squeeze it a little to make sure, but we couldn't go back to bed until we found it.

All in all, Santa rarely disappoints.

When we had children of our own, Christmas morning took on a whole new meaning. There was nothing like the kids' look when they saw all the presents for the first time. Of course, as I found out in later years, they had also been playing Christmas ninja while we were sleeping. Guess the acorn doesn't fall far from the tree.

We raised them on the magic of Santa and started our own holiday traditions. We always left cookies and milk for Santa on Christmas Eve, and he usually left them a nice thank-you note in return. More importantly, he always left them a special present.

Santa's gifts were always labeled for them to see. Initially, he would mix his unique gifts under the tree with all the others they received. During the Christmas morning carnage, the living room was strewn with torn Christmas wrapping paper and with open boxes, sometimes burying our dog, Harry. But it was always a special treat for them to come upon their special gifts from Santa.

Like I said before, Santa rarely disappoints.

As they got older, Santa hid their gifts somewhere in the house instead of under the tree. This allowed them to open all their "regular" presents first and then begin "The Great Christmas Present Search" for their special Santa present. It could be anywhere in the house, and Santa never left any clues. They had to search everywhere to find that gift. That Santa was a sly little devil, sometimes hiding the gifts in plain sight.

As we come upon another Christmas season, I'm glad that we can still believe in Santa's magic. The older you get, the fewer material things you need. Unlike what you see on TV, nobody really expects to see a car in the driveway wrapped in a bow.

If I ran into Santa at the mall tomorrow and he asked me, "What do you want for Christmas?" I'd tell him, "I just want to spend the holidays with my family." That's the only gift I need, the warmth and love that only family can provide.

And knowing Santa, he'll use his magic and come through for me again.

Santa rarely disappoints.

SHORTCUTS

- **Let Me Tell You A Story...**
   The Angel from Brooklyn 33
   The Horror of Losing Your Cell Phone 69
   My Uncle Sammy the War Hero 87
   The Night the Lights Went out in Brooklyn 121
   Understanding the Sacrifices of our Veterans 129
   The Mystery of August 14, 2003 137
   Another Summer has Come and Gone 159
   A Sandy Story 171

- **Conversation Starters**
   Marry Again? Depends on Who You Ask 57
   Make Mine a Whopper 93
   Time to Rethink How We Celebrate Weddings? 113
   Why You Should Respect the Flag 189
   What Happened to Trick or Treating? 193

- **Something to Make You Laugh**
   An Email Plea for Assistance 17
   A Few Hours at the DMV 45

My Stupid House 73
I'm Unprepared for the Apocalypse 83
Louie the Labrador Speaks Out 101
Where is My Wife? 143
The Scourge of Long Island: The Cave Cricket 147
Enough Already with Pumpkin Spice 167
My Appliances are Plotting Against Me 177
Trying the Impossible Whopper 185

- **It's All About Me**
New Year's Resolution I Can Keep 9
The "S" Word 21
A Letter to 14-Year-Old Me 25
Getting My Driver's License 29
The Burden of Paying It Forward 49
My Little League Nightmare Story 61
Good Grief, A Surprise Arrives in the Mail 109
Oh My! I Have Onychophagia 133
Where Everybody Knows Your Name 163
A Love Affair with My Snowblower 205

- **Mi Familia, Tu Familia**
My Father is Dating in Heaven 1
"Let's Be Careful Out There..." 37
The Corona Virus Hits Home 53
My Mother's Retirement Plan 65
Remembering My Father 105
My Mother's Best Halloween 181

- **Holidays**
Holiday Hangover 5
The Importance of Family Traditions 13
Celebrating Thanksgiving Italian Style 197
The Magic of Santa 213

- **Nothing Lasts Forever**
    The Death of The Caped Crusader 97
    The Loss of a Furry Friend 117
    There is Crying in Baseball 155
    Remembering John Lennon 201

- **Kids and Parenting**
    30 Years in the Blink of an Eye 41
    Vacationing With and Without the Kids 77
    Time to Leave the Nest and Fly Away 125
    Welcome to the Family 151
    You Never Stop Being a Parent, Ever 209

AFTERWORD

So that's it, dear readers.

Trying to pare down over 200 columns into this collection was more difficult than I had thought. It was kind of like bringing the kids to Sears or JCPenney for their holiday photographs. They lure you in with a price of $19.99, but you end up spending about $200.

Those retailers knew, once you saw all the beautiful pictures of your cherubic children, you were going to let them throw those pictures in the trash. You couldn't possibly walk out of there with just the two shots you get with the $19.99 package.

That's what trying to select pieces for this collection was like for me. They are all my children. I struggled with which ones to use and which ones to exclude.

I tried to select a good mix of my work to keep you entertained from start to finish. Reading my stories this way gives you a pretty good idea of my reader's experience when they get the paper every week.

When I was a kid, this was what I wanted to do with my life. I've always loved reading the newspaper, especially the columnists, as you begin to identify with them more than the reporters. A reporter tells you the story about what happened. The columnist gives you their opinion on what happened. My opinion on things has always defined my life.

Former Newsday columnist Ed Lowe had a gift for storytelling. He didn't have to manufacture stories. Ed just commented on things that were affecting his life and the lives of the people around him. He depended on his readers, family, friends, and acquaintances to bring him their stories. He had a knack for telling the story in their voice but using his words.

I loved to read what Jimmy Breslin and Pete Hamill had to say on almost any topic. Sportswriters like Dick Young and Mike Lupica (before he became political) had that same gift. They all brought a little of themselves into their stories, giving them a human touch.

The art of telling a story through a newspaper column seems to be fading into oblivion. I'd like to think what I do is keeping that type of journalism alive.

While at the dinner table or hanging out with friends and co-workers, I love bringing up a topic. I always have an opinion one way or the other, but I enjoy hearing what everyone else thinks. I'm always reading about obscure topics, so I love introducing them into a conversation. I guess I'm just curious about what is going on in the world.

Thank you for choosing to take this journey with me. I've got many more stories to tell, so maybe we can do this again sometime?

ACKNOWLEDGMENTS

While working as a sports editor for two college newspapers (Nassau Community College and The New York Institute of Technology), I always thought I would be a famous sportswriter, or at least a newspaper columnist. During those years, I've had some great editors, like Walter G. Hoefer and John Colquhoun. They gave me free rein to express my opinions while still being grammatically correct.

Alas, life got in the way and instead, I pursued a successful career in Healthcare IT.

It took almost 40 years to finally get the opportunity to express my views again. I got my restart writing for a baseball blog site called "Around the Horn," looking for someone to cover the Mets. I became friends with a few guys who were covering other teams from around the country. Joseph Botana covered the Milwaukee Brewers and Jim Tsapelas the St. Louis Cardinals. Without realizing it at first, we were the crotchety old men of the group while being surrounded by what turned out to be High School seniors, including the site administrator Kyle May. Without that group of people, I'm not sure I would have found my way back into the writing business. I'm proud to say I'm still good friends with both Joe and Jim today.

Towards the end of 2016, I saw a small advertisement in the Massapequa Observer, our local town paper, quite by accident. The subscription-based newspaper, which I did not subscribe to at the time, was delivered as an insert to home subscribers of Newsday. They were looking for someone to help write sports stories.

Johnathan Mulford was the youngest son of my brother's childhood friend Scott Mulford. He was drafted by the St. Louis Cardinals in 2016. Knowing Scott and his boys, I called him to congratulate him, and we started talking about his feelings when his son was drafted. Since Johnathan was a graduate of Massapequa High School, I thought the Observer might be interested in a local sports-related story.

I wrote an article about Johnathan being drafted, but from the parent's point of view, and submitted it to the Observer. Jennifer Fauci, the editor at the time, printed it in the next issue, then asked me to send her something else. I found it challenging to come up with another Massapequa-related sports story, so I sent a story about the rivalry between people who live in Massapequa and those from Massapequa Park.

It took a few weeks to publish that story, but they had such positive feedback from their readers, Jennifer asked me for another story.

I've been sending them stories ever since.

I've worked with several different editors in the last four years, including my current editor, Dave Gil De Rubio. Everyone at the Anton News Group, which publishes the Massapequa Observer, has always been supportive.

But no editor of my work has ever been as insightful and thorough as my wife, Barbara. Never one to sugarcoat anything; she can tell when something I write is good, or it sounds like I'm just mailing it in. If she doesn't get it, I'll rewrite it. If it makes her smile, it's good to go.

Of course, no published writer would be anywhere without a great publisher, Stephanie Larkin, and her team at Red Penguin Books. This is my second book with the penguins and I couldn't be prouder to represent them.

Writing a weekly column only works if you have an unlimited source of material to tap into. My life, on its own, is not all that interesting. However, I have many memories to draw upon and am surrounded by a large, loving family that provides me with plenty of material. My next-door neighbor Jackie gave me a coffee mug that says, "I am a writer. Anything you say or do may be used in a story." She thinks I am channeling the late Long Island columnist Ed Lowe. Now when I see her, she calls me "Ed."

I've developed a knack for taking the smallest detail and turning it into a 650-word story that I have had the pleasure of sharing with readers since 2017. Most times, I try to make you laugh or smile. One thing I promise, it will always be worth your while to take three or four minutes out of your busy day to see what is going on inside my mind.

For that, I thank you, my dear readers. Without readers, I'd just be a blogger trying to entertain myself...

ABOUT THE AUTHOR

Paul DiSclafani is an award-winning columnist for the Anton News Group, which publishes local newspapers in Nassau County on Long Island, in New York. As a weekly columnist for the Massapequa Observer since 2016, his column "Long Island Living" has garnered several writing awards.

In 2021, the Press Club of Long Island (PCLI) recognized Long Island Living as the best column on Long Island, awarding it First Place in the "Narrative-Column" category of their annual Media Awards. The competition included all Long Island based newspapers, including Newsday, which won 106 other awards. Long Island Living had been previously honored by the PCLI in both 2018 (Third Place) and 2020 (Second Place). In 2020, the New York Press Association awarded Long Island Living as one of the best humor columns in all of New York State (Third Place).

A Massapequa resident since 1967, Paul had his roots in the East New York section of Brooklyn, growing up surrounded by a large Italian family. Many of his columns and musings recall family gatherings and touch on all aspects of life today.

Paul began his love affair with the printed word after taking a journalism class during his senior year in High School. That led to a successful writing career in college as a sportswriter and editor. Although pursuing a career in the world of Healthcare IT, he continued to make friends and colleagues chuckle with stories and tales (both written and verbal) through the years.

Having told stories over the years of adventures with his friends and even chronicling them in short story form, he decided to finally sit down and write a book about one of them. "Burning Through the West Coast," his first book, was published by Red Penguin Books in October of 2020.

His work has also been published in several short story collections. Visit his website at www.pauldisclafani.com for a complete listing of all his Long Island Living columns and published works. You can also subscribe to his monthly newsletter on the web page.

A married father of two, Paul and his wife Barbara have been blessed with two great kids, James and Kevin. Paul is a member of **The Society of Professional Journalists**, the **Long Island Authors Club** and the **Long Island Writers Club**.

Awards:
• 2021 Press Club of Long Island Media Awards: Narrative-Column (Third Place) "Long Island Living"

• 2021 Press Club of Long Island Media Awards: Humor Column (Second Place) "A Few Hours at the DMV"

• 2020 Press Club of Long Island Media Awards: Narrative-Column (Second Place) "Long Island Living"

• 2020 Press Club of Long Island Media Awards: Humor Column (Third Place) "My Stupid House"

• 2020 New York Press Association: Best Humor Column (Third Place) "Long Island Living"

• 2018 Press Club of Long Island Media Awards: Narrative-Column (Third Place) "Long Island Living"

ALSO BY PAUL DISCLAFANI

PUBLICATIONS:

MEETING BRUCE SPRINGSTEEN
… and Other Tales of Debauchery
Red Penguin, 2024

Burning Through the West Coast
6,000 Miles, 576 Beers, 4 States, 3 Guys from the East Coast, and a Bag of Weed
Red Penguin, 2020

CONTRIBUTIONS TO COLLECTIONS:

A Trip for the Books
From the Red Penguin Collection (2020)

It's the End of the World
From the Red Penguin Collection (2020)

www.ingramcontent.com/pod-product-compliance
Lightning Source LLC
Chambersburg PA
CBHW072153070526
44585CB00015B/1118